Assessing the
Financial Benefits of
Human Resource
Development

New Perspectives in Organizational Learning, Performance, and Change

JERRY W. GILLEY, SERIES EDITOR

Philosophy and Practice of Organizational Learning, Performance, and Change by Jerry W. Gilley, Peter Dean, and Laura Bierema

Assessing the Financial Benefits of Human Resource Development by Richard A. Swanson

The Manager as Change Agent by Jerry W. Gilley, Scott A. Quatro, Erik Hoekstra, Doug D. Whittle, and Ann Maycunich

Assessing the Financial Benefits of Human Resource Development

Richard A. Swanson

PERSEUS PUBLISHING
Cambridge, Massachusetts

Many of the designations used by manufacturers and sellers to distinguish their products are claimed as trademarks. Where those designations appear in this book and Perseus Publishing was aware of a trademark claim, the designations have been printed in initial capital letters.

A CIP record for this book is available from the Library of Congress.
Copyright © 2001 by Richard A. Swanson
ISBN: 0-7382-0457-9

Perseus Publishing is a member of the Perseus Books Group.
Find us on the World Wide Web at http://www.perseuspublishing.com

Perseus Publishing books are available at special discounts for bulk purchases in the U.S. by corporations, institutions, and other organizations. For more information, please contact the Special Markets Department at the Perseus Books Group, 11 Cambridge Center, Cambridge, MA 02142, or call 617-252-5298.

Text design by Tonya Hahn
Set in 11-point Minion by Perseus Publishing Services

First printing, May 2001
1 2 3 4 5 6 7 8 9 10—03 02 01

Dedicated to new life and all its potential

Finn Tavis Parker
August 12, 1997

Åland Walter Rinehart
March 8, 2000

Camille Lynne Kotschevar
September 12, 2000

Publisher's Note

Organizations are living systems, in a constant state of dynamic evolution. New Perspectives in Organizational Learning, Performance, and Change is designed to showcase the most current theory and practice in human resource and organizational development, exploring all aspects of the field—from performance management to adult learning to corporate culture. Integrating cutting-edge research and innovative management practice, this library of titles will serve as an essential resource for human resource professionals, educators, students, and managers in all types of organizations.

The series editorial board includes leading academics and practitioners whose insights are shaping the theory and application of human resource development and organizational design.

Series Editor
Jerry W. Gilley, Colorado State University

Editorial Board

Contents

List of Figures

Preface

This book is for the Human Resource Development (HRD) professional who wants to be taken seriously in their organization. In that every organization is an economic entity, any organizational expenditure will be viewed as a cost to be reduced or as a means to a performance goal. Positioning HRD as a partner in achieving worthy performance goals is the orientation of this book, and getting readers to be able to assess the financial benefit of HRD interventions is the purpose of this book. The goal is that after studying this book, this is what you will be able to do.

Research on HRD practice informs us that less than 5 percent of the HRD programs that are carried out in organizations are financially assessed. This is a fundamental problem for the HRD profession. For HRD to gain its rightful status as a major organizational process—capable of improving the conditions and performance of organizations—it will need to have a track record of outcomes that represent financial benefits to its host organization. This book provides the mental model, the financial basics, and the specific tools to do this work. It quickly spans the principles and practice required to answer the following key questions:

- What is the *forecasted* financial benefit resulting from an HRD intervention?
  (Before-the-fact assessment based on forecasted financial data)
- What is the *actual* financial benefit resulting from an HRD intervention?
  (In-process assessment based on actual financial data)

- What is the *approximate* financial benefit resulting from an HRD intervention?
  (After-the-fact assessment based on approximations of actual financial data)

The Book

Chapters 1–3 of the book introduce the reader to the basic knowledge required in understanding the assessment of HRD financial benefits. Chapters 4–6 walk the reader through all the calculations required in executing the General Financial Assessment Model using specially developed financial assessment worksheets. Chapters 7–9 present case examples for *forecasting* financial benefits, determining *actual* financial benefits, and *approximating* financial benefits. Chapter 10 provides detailed advice on the presentation of financial results data to organizational decision makers. The three appendixes provide additional resources to the reader—an essay and a capsule report of actual financial studies and reproducible financial assessment forms.

It is always interesting to look back to discern how something came about. This book has three catalysts spread across four decades. The first has been the lessons learned as a young boy from my businessman father. The lessons of purposefulness and the value of planning, the lessons of costs, margins, profit percentage, and the time value of money have been wonderful gifts. To quote my father, a true gentleman and businessman not obsessed with money, "It's a way to keep score."

The second catalyst to this book came in 1973 from Gil Cullen, who was the corporate manager of training and development for Johns-Manville Corporation. As a young professor newly engaged in the preparation of HRD professionals at Bowling Green State University, I listened as he spoke of his frustration over not having the financial tools he needed to convince top management that HRD was a sound investment. After many years of experience, Cullen had come to believe that responsible HRD programs yielded performance results that paid back far more to the company than they cost. At that time he and I planned and executed a series of cost-benefit studies with the goal of establishing financial decision rules related to HRD investments.

The third catalyst to this book is a former doctoral student and colleague of mine, Deane Gradous. Deane and I have written together on a number of occasions. She has always claimed to be a better editor than a writer. Many dispute this observation, saying she is an excellent writer and an excellent editor. In 1987 she was there to help to propel an earlier version of the forecasting portion of this book at a time when I needed help.

Beyond these three people, there have been numerous professional and organizational partners that have helped advance the notion of HRD results assessment and the financial assessment of the benefits from HRD interventions. The following people have contributed in real ways to this book: Gil Cullen, Gary D. Geroy, Farhood Heidary, Elwood F. Holton III, Mitchell E. Kusy Jr., Ralph E. Long, Joseph Martelli, Brent W. Mattson, Timothy R. McClernon, Nancy R. Mosier, Brian P. Murphy, Robert J. Prifrel, Lawrence J. Quartana, Gary R. Sisson, Catherine M. Sleezer, James H. Sleezer, Barbara L. Swanson, and Richard J. Torraco.

The following organizations have contributed in real ways to this book: American Express, Arthur Andersen and Company, CIGNA, CIGNA Healthcare, CitiCorp, Control Data, GroupHealth Inc., International Society for Performance Improvement, Minnesota Mining and Manufacturing (3M), Northern States Power, Paradigm Corporation, Process Management International, Right Associates, and the University of Minnesota.

My best hope is that readers will use this book to fundamentally shift their thinking about HRD and the status of the work they do in organizations.

Richard A. Swanson
St. Paul, Minnesota
January 2001

Focusing on Financial Results from HRD Investments

Human resource development (HRD) is a process that operates within a host organization or system. The purpose of HRD almost universally revolves around learning and performance and their connection (Gilley and Maycunich, 2000; Ruona, 2000). "HRD is defined as a process of developing and unleashing human expertise through organization development and personnel training and development for the purpose of improving performance" (Swanson, 1995, 208). Although HRD is primarily defined as a process, HRD is also thought of in terms of programs, interventions, functions, departments, and job title—all of which cost money and build expectations from HRD sponsors.

When HRD is viewed as a process within a host organization it can be logically connected to the organization and its core processes, groups, and workers. Figure 1.1 provides an HRD worldview visualization useful for beginning to think about the assessment of its financial benefits. The HRD process and process phases (analyze, propose, create, implement, and assess) are imbedded in the host organization's inputs, processes, and outputs. HRD that has clear financial benefits works in partnership with the core processes of an organization that are focused on producing mission-related goods and services having value to customers. Much of the activity of HRD is spent on performance drivers versus actual performance. Thus, HRD uses interventions like executive coaching, system redesign, team building, training of expertise, action research, and valuing diversity as means to a performance goal, not as a goal in itself.

1

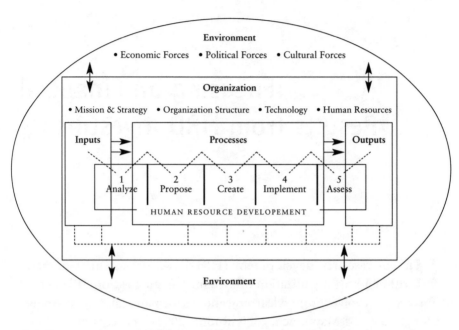

FIGURE 1.1   System Worldview of Human Resource Development

Organizations (with some exceptions) are not in the business of valuing diversity, building employee expertise, e-learning, or establishing well-functioning work teams. They do these things to achieve other goals. That is why they are called performance drivers (Holton, 1999; Kaplan and Norton, 1996). A performance driver that is not connected to performance goals and the variables needed to achieve them is generally ineffective and could even be harmful. For example, team building can be thought of as a good idea only when it is used in the right situation. In the wrong situation, implementing team building could cost a great deal and end up lowering work group and organization performance. Thus, HRD analysis and assessment phases are critical in assessing the financial benefits of HRD. The HRD worldview model is essential in supporting the following generalizations:

1. The up-front HRD analysis phase and the final HRD assessment phase should be connected to the fundamental mission and outputs of the organization.

2. HRD analysis and assessment phases should be directly connected. The performance requirements determined in the analysis phase should be the focus of the performance outcomes measured in the assessment phase.
3. Assessing financial benefits of HRD requires attention to the organization's mission-related outputs in terms of the goods and services it produces.

Mission-Related Outputs

Performance is assessed at various levels: the organization, work process, group, and individual contributor levels (Rummler and Brache, 1995; Swanson and Holton, 2001). Furthermore, *performance* can be thought of as mission-related outputs in the form of goods or services produced at the various levels (organization, work process, group, and individual contributor). For example:

Durable goods (hard goods): Televisions, door hinges, cellular phones
Nondurable goods: Bread, news magazines, undershirts
Organizational services: Organizational culture surveys, financial audits, parking lot maintenance
Personal services: Therapeutic massage, retirement planning, child care

Each of these outputs can be easily converted into money. Thus, the more closely an HRD intervention is connected to mission-related outputs that can be measured and monetized, the easier it is to engage in financial assessment.

When the HRD process is central to an organization, it is logically and operationally connected to mission-level outputs of its host organization. In other words, HRD demonstrates that it can work with core organizational processes and contribute to core performance requirements at various performance levels.

The state of HRD practice in terms of financial assessment is appalling. Practitioners report that they financially assess only 3 percent of their HRD programs (Bassi et al., 1996). Since every organization is an economic entity (including nonprofit and public-sector organizations), this state of affairs fundamentally marginalizes the HRD profession. Most HRD professionals try to argue that HRD interventions will make and have made positive differences in performance. They do this without presenting financial forecasts of performance or verifying after-the-fact financial performance.

Managing strictly by the financial numbers is not what is being suggested. There has been a legitimate reaction to management's use of single-dimension financial measures. Most notably, *The Balanced Scorecard* (Kaplan and Norton, 1996) has been proposed instead as a responsible organizational measure for decision making. They suggest measuring the domains of the customer, learning and growth, the internal business process, and financial results. The balanced scorecard for HRD includes financial performance along with assessment of learning and perceptions (Swanson and Holton, 1999). In the past the HRD profession has relied almost solely on the least valid and least useful measure—perceptions in the form of participant reactions. Even more absurd has been the reliance on participant self-ratings of their learning (which is invalid) and participant perceptions of financial results from HRD programs (invalid) (see Alliger et al., 1997; Dixon, 1990; Holton, 1997).

Financial benefit assessment is a method for making decisions about HRD investments. The method is similar to the analytical methods that managers use to decide which products to develop and what equipment to purchase, as well as whether to expand or relocate facilities. If making decisions about major investments in organizational assets deserves thorough analysis, then making decisions about HRD investments merits the same thorough analysis. Most professionals would agree that HRD programs represent major outlays of organizational resources. For this reason, decisionmakers require information about an HRD program's expected and actual impact on organizational finances. Lacking sufficient or accurate information, decisionmakers could fail to support HRD programs that have the potential to produce significant benefits for the organization. For this and other business reasons, assessing financial benefits is potentially the most strategic skill that the HRD professional can acquire. If the results of HRD programs are forecasted and assessed in financial terms and reported to organization leaders, HRD will likely gain top management's enthusiastic commitment. HRD and management will become true partners in seeking and reaching organizational goals. Performance is the key, and financially valuing that performance is the essential assessment method.

Framework for Assessing Financial Benefits

The framework and key questions for assessing the financial benefits of HRD is illustrated in Figure 1.2. This framework displays the three financial benefit assessment methods presented in this book. The financial benefit assessment methods are focused on *forecasted actual*, or *approximated* data. The initiation of the assessment of financial benefits can be *before* the implementation, *during* the HRD process, or *after* the implementation of the HRD intervention. The key questions provide three variations on the assessment of financial benefits of HRD.

- What is the *forecasted* financial benefit resulting from an HRD intervention?
  (Before-the-fact assessment based on forecasted financial data.)
- What is the *actual* financial benefit resulting from an HRD intervention?
  (In-process assessment based on actual financial data.)
- What is the *approximate* financial benefit resulting from an HRD intervention?
  (After-the-fact assessment based on approximations of actual financial data.)

Illustrations of Practice

Recently Walt Godfrey, HRD manager of a local corporation, wanted help in preparing for his upcoming meeting with the chief executive officer and two vice presidents of his corporation. Believe it or not, in his six years as HRD manager, Walt had never seriously read his company's annual report, let alone scheduled a meeting with anybody to discuss how the HRD department could contribute to corporate earnings. Two months before his big meeting, Walt asked me for information to assess

Initiation of the Financial Assessment

		Before-the-Fact ⟶ During-the-Process ⟶ After-the-Fact		
	Forecasted	What is the *Forecasted* Financial Benefit?		
Assessing Financial Benefit Methods	Actual		What is the *Actual* Financial Benefit?	
	Approximate			What is the *Approximate* Financial Benefit?

FIGURE 1.2 Framework and Key Questions for Assessing HRD Financial Benefits

the financial benefits of HRD. He read and learned; his transformation was quick. Walt was crossing the threshold to become a true business partner with his company, and he wanted some last-minute reassurance. Walt's proposal to management was solid. He identified a critical performance need within the organization and spelled out a realistic performance goal. He forecasted the financial benefits and clearly documented them. I was not surprised, later in the week, to hear that management had approved Walt's business proposal.

In many struggling companies executives have come to view HRD as an essential business function with the purpose of increasing corporate earnings through cost-effective organizational development and employee training. HRD professionals want to exert more influence in their organizations and management wants them to make greater contributions. The efforts of those who can handle the pressure are paying off in increased responsibility for HRD departments and greater earnings for their organizations. As regional, national, and worldwide competition becomes more intense, corporate leaders will increasingly recognize that employees are resources that must be maintained and developed. Managers are learning that investing in HRD is as important as investing in new technologies. They are finding that it does an organization little good to invest in sophisticated systems if employees can neither understand these systems nor operate the new technologies within their work environments. High-level individual, work group, and organization performances are the key, and responsible HRD programs focus on increasing those performances.

The following demands for human resource development that will have to be met in the next decade illustrate the size of the challenge:

- Assisting organizations in shaping their systems for high performance
- Developing millions of managers
- Developing millions of current workers who need to learn new skills
- Orienting and training millions of new employees

The American Society for Training and Development estimates that American employers annually spend over $50 billion on programs to develop their employees. When the value of the work time that employees expend in HRD is included in these estimates, the cost of HRD doubles. As far back as 1984 the U.S. government indicated that about 36 million, or approximately 33 percent of all employed people, received either formal company training or information or on-the-job training (U.S. Bureau of the Census, 1984) and this percentage keeps growing. Given such a high level of corporate concern and investment, it is no wonder that organizations want their HRD professionals to think like businesspeople—not like therapists, teachers, or record keepers.

When decisionmakers decide to spend large sums of money on HRD, they seek to evaluate HRD program options much as they evaluate other large investments, that is, on the basis of financial returns to the organization. It therefore follows that employee development efforts, for the most part, should be tied to the profit-making goals and performance plans of the organization, whether it be profitmaking or in the public sector. Wherever underperforming employees reduce the organization's productivity, everyone suffers. The public will be poorly served, market share will be lost, and the organization's earnings will be diminished. For these and other reasons, HRD decisions made outside of the performance-profit frame of reference are open to question. But if decisions are made within this frame of reference, HRD becomes an important means for meeting the goals of the organization, whether they are for profit or for service.

HRD professionals can contribute to changing technologies at work, can help people perform new job tasks, and can overcome the disaffection that workers at all levels feel between themselves and their organization. HRD professionals can be prepared to prove to management that their programs will raise organizational performance. Such proof is developed by calculating accurate, meaningful baseline measures of performance and relating any expected increases in these measures to specific HRD programs. To demonstrate the relationships between HRD and improvements in performance or profit, HRD professionals must learn to use financial analysis methods similar to those used for making capital investment decisions. Remember, work performance—individual or group—is the key, and forecasting benefits of changing work performance is the subject of this book.

Bottom-Line Orientation

Depreciation schedules, returns on investments, and payback periods have been used for decades for calculating investments in capital goods. Decisionmakers use these valuable tools selectively because they have not had an equivalent forecasting tool for analyzing potential investments in human capital. As a consequence of the lack of a standardized method, most decisionmakers have failed to consider fully the financial consequences of their HRD policies and decisions. Typically, managers fall back on using only cost questions when they budget for HRD: "How much will it cost?" "How much did we spend last year?" "How much do we want to spend this year?"

Because they apply only cost questions to their HRD programs, most decisionmakers fail to recognize HRD's strategic contributions to the organization. Inevitably, they view the company's HRD department as a costly burden rather than the means for obtaining higher levels of valuable performance. We should not be surprised to find managers in organizations of all sizes and types making tough HRD decisions without benefit of a financial benefit assessment tool. The following examples are typical:

- A medium-size manufacturing company producing electronic circuit boards earned steady profits. Even with high rates of employee turnover and rejection of product, the company continued to make money. The management group had never considered the possibility of investing in HRD. Thus, spending any money at all on HRD would be a significant departure from normal company practice. When a consultant proposed that the company invest $20,000 in training ten assembly workers, management wondered at the extravagance. The management group was unaware that in just forty days this investment could return over $200,000.

- Recently, the executive vice presidents of a *Fortune* 100 company instituted a new approach to developing their workforce. Their stable, experienced, and productive workforce had always learned how to do their jobs through trial and error. A thorough cost-benefit analysis showed that significant increases in employee work performance could be expected to result from a formal innovative program of supervisory development. Eventually, the financial benefits actually realized from just four offerings of the innovative program more than matched the forecasted benefits expected from thirty groups of supervisors. Not surprisingly, the executive vice presidents have chosen to institute HRD investments right along with their capital investments throughout the organization.

- In yet another instance, a corporate manager of HRD had to choose one program from among several optional programs designed to develop new work attitudes and new initiatives in the current workforce. The proposed HRD program could be produced by an in-house staff, by several HRD vendors, or by two public educational institutions. Which one should be chosen to do the project?

Decisionmakers face a major difficulty. Their understanding of the economics of HRD as a major factor in increasing the value of human capital in their organizations is limited. Attention to the economics of specific HRD programs is rare. Searches through the literature on organization development and employee training and development yield little on the subject of assessing the financial benefits of HRD activities. Lacking appropriate analysis tools, decisionmakers attempt to apply to HRD the cost-benefit analysis tools that they have traditionally applied to capital investments, despite the fact that human competence does not depreciate on a scheduled basis. In fact, human knowledge, attitudes, and skills can be expected to grow. Human development often works like a chain reaction; get good people started in the right direction, and they will tend to continue on that path.

Playing by Corporate Rules

Companies exist to make profits through the work performances of competent employees. By establishing goals and strategies, decisionmakers determine what individual, group, or organizational work performances will be pursued. At the level of strategic planning, executives may invest in improving organizational performance through HRD or through such other measures as marketing, new equipment purchases, expanded sales regions, or mergers and acquisitions. HRD managers carefully allocate scarce organizational resources (financial or human) with the expectation of attaining their goals. But the very idea of being held financially accountable for HRD investment decisions can be threatening. How do they know what is the "right" decision when investing in human resources? In the past, HRD managers turned to traditional training and development evaluation methods. Evaluation of learning is not new; educational institutions have been evaluating student learning for decades. But the business perspective on evaluating worker performance and other HRD outcomes is different. In business and industry, HRD outcomes are measured in dollars and cents. In the public sector, HRD outcomes are measured in terms of service. The business perspective on evaluating worker learning is different because here decisionmakers focus on the results of applying the expertise rather than on the expertise itself. Such applications of expertise lead to improved performance and to increased organizational prestige or earnings.

HRD may be viewed as a business process that converts inputs into outputs. Employee work performances that contribute to the goals of the organization are the outputs. Economic analysis of HRD can be used to decide whether to invest in an HRD program and whether to continue an HRD program. It can also be used to decide between HRD program methods for achieving the same performance goals. Finally, it can help determine which participant groups actually achieved the highest or most valuable performance goals. HRD programs are usually evaluated after organizational resources have been committed and consumed. Such after-the-fact evaluation offers hindsight, but it usually contributes little toward increasing decisionmakers' confidence about returns on HRD investments to be made in the future unless these results are regularly reported. Financial forecasting and actual results are needed. The financial benefits assessment method is an essential tool for analyzing and choosing among optional HRD expenditures in organizations: It makes it possible to answer important economic questions.

What Is the Gain?

It is important for you, the HRD professional, to understand the relationship between what you do and the financial benefits you produce for your company. HRD financial benefit forecasting is a tool that will allow you to connect a sound performance need with a sound HRD solution to that need.

With this tool you, the HRD manager, will be willing to be held accountable for the programs of your HRD department. If and when you are asked about what you do, you will have ample evidence of the value of your HRD activities—that is, if you begin now to use the tool to analyze performance problems and the benefits that result from the HRD solutions to those problems.

With HRD financial benefit assessment, you have the means to show decisionmakers in your company how to value HRD. You and the executive decisionmakers have the means to help people grow and to make strategic choices about the HRD department. Moreover, you and the executive decisionmakers have the means to evaluate potential solutions to organizational problems that may have been overlooked or undervalued.

As you will note throughout this book, I take the position that "strategic" HRD generally results in the greatest benefit for the organization (Torraco and Swanson, 1995). Being strategic almost always requires a planned, systematic response to a present or future performance goal and relies on a structured, up-front analysis (see Swanson, 1996).

HRD interventions are often inappropriately proposed as solutions to ill-defined problems or as a weak solution to a performance problem that can be better solved through direct management action. In such less-strategic applications of HRD, the financial benefit assessment method will yield results that are borderline or negative—exactly the kind of information you need to keep you from making the big mistake of investing in structured HRD that is incapable of improving performance.

Conclusion

Here is a summary of the chapter's key points:

- All organizations are economic entities.
- HRD needs to be connected to mission-related outputs of its host organization.
- Performance is the key and financially valuing that performance is the method.
- The balanced scorecard for HRD includes the results domains of performance (financial), learning, and perceptions.
- A framework for assessment of financial benefits includes *forecasted, actual,* and *approximated* benefits.
- Strategic HRD requires a planned, systematic response to performance goals and a financial assessment.

Financial Assessment Basics

For most HRD professionals, assessing the financial benefits of HRD programs represents an undeveloped area of expertise in most HRD professionals. It possibly also represents a new role for the HRD department in implementing organizational strategy (Torraco and Swanson, 1995). The purpose of this chapter is to develop an understanding of the role that financial assessment can have in planning for and documenting HRD benefits in any organization and to introduce the assessment of financial benefits from multiple perspectives. The following case is based on a real-world situation.

The HRD Fantasy

Barb Thompson's HRD department didn't make it through the reorganization intact. A confident director of HRD, Barb had a smooth-running operation. Only recently, the HRD department's executive advisory committee had evaluated and approved a new corporate executive development program. Barb seemed to be doing all that could be expected of a director of HRD in a *Fortune* 100 corporation.

A capital-intensive organization, this company employed a relatively small workforce. Employees who were selected for participation in HRD programs immediately found themselves on the fast track, receiving quick promotions and[1] generous rewards for their efforts. The HRD de-

---

[1]Note: Human capital theory is at the root economic theory for those who study human contributions to the economics of systems. The classic study of the consequences of investing in a person's knowledge and expertise was first published by Gary S. Becker in 1964, Human Capital: A Theoretical and Empirical Analysis, with Special Reference to Education.

partment enjoyed being a part of and promoting the good times. Years ago, Barb purposefully had chosen to maintain a supportive role and a "corporate perk" atmosphere for her HRD department. She handled her leadership role with a blend of dignity and celebration, and her department had been successful for some time.

Then the economy took a sudden nosedive, and Barb's seemingly strong and impervious department went down with it. Easy growth had caused many of the company's operations to become soft and overgrown—it doesn't take long. Barb's department, as a promoter of good times, had little to offer her company when it encountered difficult times. In less than six months, Barb's highly polished staff of ten was reduced to Barb and one administrative assistant. During the corporatewide reduction in the workforce, it was not clear to top management that the HRD department could address the fundamental issues of the business. And in such times the fundamentals are all that matter.

Even if the HRD department had focused on the economics of the business, it probably would have been somewhat reduced in size. Without exception, all departments had experienced cuts in staff, but what hurt the most was that the goals of the HRD department weren't really given serious consideration when the cuts were made. Barb had believed all along that her department was making important contributions to the company. Now she suddenly had come face-to-face with management's perception of her department's minimal worth to the company. Ironically, just two months before, Barb had emphatically rejected an offer from an expert consultant in financial assessment to help her and her staff talk to top management about the economics of the HRD department. Barb confidently reported to the consultant that HRD received wonderful support from top management. Further, she thought that discussion about the financial contributions of HRD was not necessary. When the HRD department finally did hear about its worth from top management, it was too late. Barb's perception of top management's support for the HRD department had been a fantasy.

Exploding HRD Myths

A number of value-laden myths have entered the HRD profession. These myths may have been partially the result of HRD's having taken on too many "it feels good" goals without performing thorough performance and work analyses to back up their HRD programs. Some myths that have haunted HRD include:

1. Social pressure is the basis of HRD.
2. Managers don't care about HRD.
3. HRD costs too much.
4. You can't quantify the benefits of HRD.

These myths should be exploded. Hard economic thinking and even harder planning are what is required, not mythology. HRD professionals should be businesspersons first and HRD specialists second (see Appendix A: "Everything Important in Business and Industry Is Evaluated"). This shift in perspective is the first step in exploding the HRD myths. The four HRD myths will disintegrate when the transition to thorough performance analysis and financial assessment becomes commonplace.

Myth 1: Social Pressure Is the Basis of HRD.   A quick look around the corporate world will reveal organization development interventions, personnel training and development programs, and other HRD efforts that were put into place because "everyone else is doing it." Perhaps some companies get trapped in this game in the same way that some parents are trapped by their children's wanting things because other children have them. Perhaps some HRD managers have used such childish threats with management as "the company across the street has one and so should we."

I have heard talk within the HRD profession about "employee rights to development," along with statements that "HRD is a corporate perk." This kind of rhetoric seems to suggest that social pressure is the basis of HRD. But isn't it interesting that HRD professionals in organizations that strongly support HRD programs rarely, if ever, use social pressure? Most organizational decision makers who actively support HRD view it in terms of the business, the core work processes, the outcomes, and anticipating economic gains or averting economic risks.

Myth 2: Most Managers Do Not Care About HRD.   Because so few managers defend their HRD departments, ask for their help, or sing their praises, HRD professionals could easily come to believe that this myth must be true. Simultaneously, the same managers consult with others in the company about such important issues as developing workforce expertise, motivation, and aptitude and how to design work so people can be more effective in their jobs.

Never make the mistake of confusing management's caring about HRD issues with their caring about the HRD department. Furthermore, I urge you to acknowledge that the hardworking managers in your company put themselves on the line every day. Right or wrong, most managers will rely on what they believe to be their best and most trusted sources of help. Even though your HRD department may not have earned such "best" or "trusted" labels, this does not mean that most managers don't care about HRD. Managers do care about HRD. But to be a "best" and "trusted" source of know-how requires the HRD department to have a credible HRD process, including a results assessment system (Swanson and Holton, 1999).

Myth 3: HRD Costs Too Much. Good HRD generally costs a fair amount of money. Most worthwhile projects in an organization cost a fair amount of money. Usually management decides to spend available dollars on equipment, services, and projects that will give it the best return on its investment. Whenever something must be purchased that apparently will have little effect on the business, management will request the one with the lowest price.

The following example will have a familiar ring: If low-quality mailing envelopes will do the job, management tends to say, "Get them as cheaply as you can." If these inexpensive envelopes later stick together or will not feed through the postage machine, or if they make the organization look tacky in the eyes of customers, management then will tend to say, "Stop buying such junk." Conversely, if the most expensive envelopes are the kind that seal automatically and thus increase output or if they catch the attention of potential customers and bring increased sales, management will tend to say, "Get a good price if you can, but we want the best."

Cost figures by themselves are irrelevant. Reviewing HRD costs without also reviewing the associated benefits is not smart. Analyzing what you get for your money *is* smart. What most HRD managers fail to realize is that organizational decision makers usually focus only on HRD costs. When they lack information about the economic benefits of HRD, many decision makers decide consciously or unconsciously that a proposed HRD program is just another HRD program—just as an envelope is only an envelope. "So get the cheapest one."

Myth 4: You Cannot Quantify the Benefits of HRD. Listening to people find excuses why something cannot be done is always interesting. Rationalizing that the benefits of HRD cannot be quantified has kept the HRD profession in the dark ages of organizational performance. Do you suppose that management knows how many products it will sell next year? Of course not. If it knew the exact figures ahead of time, it would make exactly that many products. But because management does not know precisely how many products it will sell, it gathers the best estimates it can find and makes its decision without the satisfaction of knowing it is right. This process takes knowledge of past results, intelligence, and guts—not perfection. Likewise, a record of assessed benefits, a little more intelligence, and a lot more guts on the part of HRD professionals will explode this last myth.

There is a strong possibility that all four of these myths have arisen from inside the HRD profession. If decision makers have also learned these HRD myths, they probably learned them from HRD people. Executives, as masters of change and opportunity, have the right to expect HRD departments to join them in their struggle to achieve quality and profitability. Most decision makers are not enemies of HRD. They want to be business partners and to reap the added value that HRD can provide to the organization. All four HRD myths stand in the way of this partnership.

No Need—No Benefit

The real pressure for HRD activity will come as the result of identifying critical performance requirements. Good performance analyses are the basis of making financial benefit assessments. Management, HRD staff, a consultant, or a team can conduct a thorough performance analysis. Identifying less-than-obvious corporate needs requires gathering critical data from corporate production records, employees, customers, and the like. Even the more obvious gaps, such as the need for communication skills, would benefit from a thorough performance analysis. Analysis will ensure that an HRD program closely fits the development requirements of a specific executive group in a specific corporation. Too often, HRD programs, expensive or not, fail to deliver what is required. They deliver what they promise and still miss the need. Because conducting a good performance analysis is essential to creating value through HRD, consult some of the helpful works available (Robinson and Robinson, 1995; Rummler and Brache, 1995; Swanson, 1996).

A major practical issue in most organizations is how to distinguish between *wants* and *requirements*. What managers want is not always what they need or require. Performance variables are critical conditions that organizations must meet to achieve their performance goals and mission. The relationship between benefits assessment and performance requirements is important. *Wants* are not so important. The most important HRD skill is to be able to work with decision makers to discover genuine organizational performance requirements and to convince them that they *want* what they *need*. This goal is best accomplished by working in partnership with managers rather than by making high-pressure attempts to sell faddish HRD programs.

HRD *wants* are easy to identify and to sell to decision makers: "What do you want?" "Is this what I heard you ask for?" "Okay then, here is the program you wanted." "Are you satisfied with what we gave you?" Filling such wants is a relatively safe process. But in doing so, it is easy to ignore your organization's mission, performance goals, and performance deficiencies. The outcome of an HRD program that addresses an organizational performance goal is valuable to the extent that it closes the gap. Some HRD analysts believe that organizational requirements are more complex than wants. I don't necessarily agree. Satisfying performance requirements is just riskier. And with greater risk comes the potential for greater gains—gains for the HRD department and for the organization.

The outcome of a particular HRD program is valuable only if it is connected to an organizational performance requirement and the core processes designed to achieve those performances. A high-cost HRD program does not always result in a performance gain, whereas a low-cost HRD program may result in a large performance gain. Determining the critical performance to be attained and its value to the organization should precede the step of analyzing the costs of the HRD program. Why bother with costs if there is not a worthwhile gain within reach?

Conducting a thorough performance analysis is important, but the question "When is enough, enough?" will inevitably be raised. Enough investigation is enough when HRD professionals feel comfortable with the answers to the following questions:

- Have we identified a performance that is important to management?
- Will the HRD program positively influence that performance?
- Can we deliver a high-quality HRD program?
- Will the right people in the organization participate in and support the HRD program?

It goes without saying that assessing the financial benefits of various HRD program options will help all concerned along the path to making better decisions. An important component of any performance needs assessment is the HRD financial benefit proposal to be presented to management.

Connecting Needs with Benefits

The outcomes of HRD programs are valuable only to the extent that they are connected to specific organizational performance requirements. Additionally, HRD programs must have integrity and quality or they will not deliver the expected benefits. The basic economic issue of investing in HRD is the same as that of investing in other forms of capital. The question is one of return on investment. Will investments in people net the kinds of returns—and magnitude of returns—that the organization is seeking? Strategic opportunities, issues, costs, and profits are basically the same for investing in HRD as they are for investing in capital assets. In a competitive market, the organization must fully use its human resources to maximize its bottom-line results. In the nonprofit or government worlds, the organization must use its human resources to provide more or better service with limited resources.

Decision makers have three possible options with which to address an organizational requirement for competent human resources. The first option is to retain the existing group and initiate HRD programs such as retraining or system changes to develop and unleash the worker competence they need. The second option is to fire the existing group and acquire a new one that possesses the requisite expertise, capacity, and motivation. With this option, the issues of supply and demand for labor are similar to those for any other market commodity. The third option is to try to foresee the implications of current and future economic, social, and political forces, to consider the limited available organizational strategies, and then to choose whether to go out of business, seek out a more favorable labor market, automate, or outsource.

The HRD bias is toward the first option. Evidence can be gathered to indicate whether various work performances in the organization, especially the poorer performances, can be improved through HRD programs. Such evidence is gathered through the aforementioned performance needs assessment process. After this assessment has identified which specific work performances may be addressed wholly or in part by HRD programs, the task of forecasting HRD costs and benefits becomes an essential element of the decisionmaking process along with follow-up assessment of the actual financial results. Before exploring the specifics of this task, however, it is important to gain a historical perspective on HRD investments.

HRD Role Shift

Recent shifts in world economics have made severe inroads into the former preeminence of American industries and businesses. This is especially true for low-skill, labor-intensive industries. The transfer of what were once American jobs to offshore locations has triggered numerous social and political reactions. These reactions have ranged from instituting protectionist legislation to negotiating new labor contracts that mandate job protection and retraining. Offsetting the loss of American jobs are the short-lived advantages held by those relatively few organizations with new technologies.

Today, as never before, new and evolving technologies can be speedily replicated. New applications for current technologies are discovered at an ever-accelerating rate. An organization decides to invest in new technologies when it perceives that its competitors in a given market have access to the same technologies for the same relative cost. Failure to invest in appropriate capital assets and technologies can therefore quickly lead to the loss of an organization's competitive position in the marketplace. At the same time, investment in new technology alone cannot ensure economic success. The critical competitive edge in many organizations lies in the effectiveness and efficiency with which its workers implement and maintain corporate technologies. Two organizational variables that influence efficiency and effectiveness of performance are the attributes of the organizations themselves and the expertise of their workers. Viewed from this perspective, HRD quickly becomes the priority investment option because it will lead to desired worker, work group, work process, or organizational performances that will, in turn, yield a competitive return on investment. Although the notion that new technologies and employee expertise can be purchased as commodities may be disliked by some, such is the economic reality of some very successful organizations.

Cost-Only View of HRD

Human capital has been defined as an individual's capacity to produce goods and services (Carnevale, 1983). Individuals, firms, and societies invest in people—in human capital—to enhance and maintain individual, work group, work process, organizational, and societal capabilities. The challenge has been extended to HRD to assist organizations in carrying out their missions. HRD departments have achieved a high degree of visibility in recent years. An organization's ability to respond to rapid market and technological changes depends a great deal on the capacity of its personnel to assimilate new knowledge and skills. Directed change, however small, is seldom accomplished without costs. This is true whether the change is a matter of investing in capital assets or in human resource development. Assessing whether costly HRD programs are wasteful frills or essential strategies is possible only if their relative effectiveness is known. Before addressing the issue of costs and effectiveness, however, the more common ways to think about costs and HRD will be reviewed.

Unplanned, unstructured HRD has long been considered the most cost-effective of HRD programs. Why is this? Because most managers do not associate costs with organizational changes that evolve without benefit of planning or with changes that are gradually forced on an organization by external pressures. The "hassles" associated with change are frequently accepted by managers as the normal inefficiencies of doing business. In contrast, most managers tend to view *planned* HRD programs as incurring costs, costs that must be accounted for in their operating budgets. Such thinking leads to the question: If an organization can attain desired changes in performance without incurring any perceived costs, why should management bother to invest in HRD? What these managers fail to consider is that any less-than-optimal performance in an organization is in a real sense a loss to that organization. It costs. For example, poorly made products and poorly performed services can be thought of as economic losses to the organization. Such thinking is a departure from the cost-only perspective that is more usual in making decisions about HRD programs. Thus, although unstructured HRD may cost the least, it generally is not the most cost-effective option.

These are the three most common cost questions in reference to HRD programs: "How much does it cost?" "How much did we spend last year?" "How much do we want to spend this year?" This cost-only perspective yields very different decisions than the perspective of assessing the financial benefits to be gained from each HRD investment.

Benefit Aspect of Cost–Benefit Analysis

Cost-benefit analysis usually presumes that, given the cost of an investment and the value of the resulting change, the benefit can be determined. Current management thinking about the benefits to be derived from investments is rooted in traditional models for investing in capital assets. The benefit of any capital investment is generally expressed as the value of achieving some additional organization output over some period of time. Alternatively, it may be expressed as a ratio of the value of some additional output to the cost needed to achieve that output. Most capital investment models take into account such factors as depreciation and inflation.

In this traditional approach to thinking about expected investment benefits, two ideas are evident. First, the direct output to be derived from the investment is the focus of the analysis. If a machine is to be purchased, the decision maker looks at its potential output. If a building is planned, the decision maker looks at its potential contribution to organizational output. Second is the notion that the change that results from the investment will have value to the organization.

The cost-benefit analysis of HRD programs that is described in this book honors much of this traditional thinking about capital investment, but it entails a few major departures from the normal method of analysis. One departure is the need to recognize that the value of a human being does not depreciate. HRD investments actually constitute a relatively stable form of value added to the organization. A second departure is that the focus of the analysis of benefits expected to result from HRD activities may be quite broad. Many HRD programs focus on providing or enhancing the technical skills and knowledge that will allow individuals or groups to produce more effectively or efficiently on the job. Quite often, however, the impact of newly acquired knowledge and expertise will be of an abstract nature, such that it can best be anticipated as desired changes in the work performances of the peers or the subordinates of the people who participate in the HRD activity. For example, the performance of a group may be expected to improve as the direct result of new skills to be learned when their supervisor enrolls in an HRD program. Or perhaps a drop in worker turnover caused by a disagreeable management style is the expected performance result of an organizational development intervention with the plan management group.

A third departure from standard investment models is the period of time on which the analysis of future benefits focuses. The analysis of benefit from HRD is limited to the *period* during which several alternative HRD programs could be implemented to bring about the same change in performance. As I have stated, conducting a thorough performance analysis is important. A performance analysis will help to identify any performance discrepancies that may have HRD solutions. It also will help to identify alternative HRD program options that could achieve the same desired change in performance. If several optional HRD programs can be expected to yield the same end-performance results, then the key variable in the HRD financial assessment model will be the length of time each program takes to achieve the desired performance (Figure 2.1).

The fourth and most significant departure from standard investment thinking is the difficulty of defining the specific benefit to be derived from particular HRD investment. In traditional capital investment

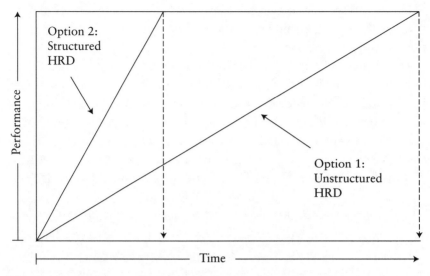

FIGURE 2.1   Time-Performance Graph

models, the benefit is the value of the additional products or services produced. In the HRD benefit assessment model, the specific benefit to be derived is the value of future changes in performance after the costs to achieve that change are deducted. The idea suggests that cost-benefit analysis of HRD programs requires a third component, namely, the value of the additional performance or the change in performance that is expected. This third component in the HRD benefit assessment model is called the *performance value.*

Performance Value

Improvements in organizational performance can best be effected by investing in capital assets, by investing in human capital through programs of selection and HRD, or by investing in some integrated combination of capital assets and HRD. Thus, changing worker or work group performance to fill an organizational need is only one strategy for an organization's survival.

In many organizational situations, the desired performance change is an *increase* in quantity of a valued output or activity. For example, the goal of HRD in a research organization may be to increase the number of patents granted per researcher or the goal of an HRD program in a chain of hotels might be to increase the number of regular customers retained. Desired performance may be a *decrease* in quantity of an unwanted output or activity and these numbers need to be refocused to the positives.

When looking at performances expected to change as a result of HRD programs, the analyst must focus on the baseline performance level, which is the measure of performance prior to the HRD program. The desired performance level is the level of performance expected to occur as a direct result of the HRD program. In some cases an HRD program may begin before the performance of the target group or organization begins. An orientation program for new workers is an example. But an HRD program could also begin whenever the target group or organization performs at a level lower than the desired performance goal. This would be the usual situation whenever a system, a procedure, or the structure of the organization is to be changed. For example, HRD activities may focus on team building and negotiating leadership roles in newly structured groups. In this situation, the aim of the HRD program might be to reach a specified performance goal by developing efficient communications, clarifying decisionmaking responsibilities, and retaining valued workers. The gain in performance from the baseline level to the desired level will be valued and included in the HRD return-on-investment analysis.

HRD Benefit Assessment Model

Several models for assessing the financial benefit of HRD programs have been available to decision makers for some time (Mosier, 1990). The three most commonly used models are return on investment, benefit-cost ratio, and payback period. These models appeal to decision makers because they are familiar with them. Many managers have grown accustomed to using such models to assess the value of investing in capital assets. Some managers have been applying these investment models to the task of evaluating the actual results of HRD programs, but not to forecasting the expected results.

One unknown variable in forecasting the results of an HRD program may account for the lack of forecasting in organizations. That variable is the length of time that the returns from one program option will be effective in comparison with the length of time that all other available options will be effective. Another problem with using financial models to forecast the benefits of HRD is the difficulty in assigning a dollar value to qualitative benefits. Any way they are figured, the numbers used to represent the costs and benefits of HRD may never provide a complete picture of the value of a proposed program. There may be many non-quantitative outcomes that should, but will not, be considered. These include such "ceremonial" effects of HRD as employee recognition, the company's reputation for caring about its workers, and the general quality of life at work. Given these constraints, the goal of conducting an objective cost-benefit analysis of an HRD program can become an interesting challenge.

In the following chapters I provide the analyst with strategies for quantifying these difficult qualitative dimensions. The model presented does not view benefits as the value of the change in performance but rather as the value of the change in performance minus the costs incurred to achieve that change. The model takes into account existing performance levels and any changes in performance that may be brought about as a result of both HRD and non-HRD activities.

The basic financial assessment model will be described in detail in following chapters. It includes methods for determining monetary values for the following components: the *performance value* resulting from the HRD program, the *cost* of the HRD program, and the *benefit* resulting from the HRD program. The HRD financial assessment model is simplicity itself:

Performance Value (performance value resulting from HRD intervention)
– Cost (cost of the HRD intervention)
Benefit (benefit is the performance value minus the cost)

Forecasted Versus Actual Assessments

It is relatively straightforward to determine the financial benefits of an HRD program once the effort has been completed. But it is often a little more difficult to forecast and choose the best among several HRD program options for achieving a desired performance goal. It may be even more difficult to choose between several HRD program options and several non-HRD options.

Results assessment examines the actual *effects* of a program (Swanson and Holton, 1999; Swanson and Sawzin, 1975; Parker, 1986). Forecasting in the financial realm develops economic data for *making choices* between HRD program options and between HRD and non-HRD options. The financial forecasting assessment supports forward-looking, decisionmaking processes. The goal is to make better HRD decisions before investing in programs, rather than to wait to evaluate HRD after the investments have been made. Both are important.

The forecasting task is performed by the analyst as the last step in the performance analysis process. It is an essential part of making proposals to management. Although this book concentrates on assessing financial benefits to be derived from HRD programs, the general benefits assessment model is equally powerful for forecasting financial data and determining the actual financial effects of HRD programs.

The usefulness of any forecasting model in the decisionmaking process is dependent on its capacity for enhancing human capabilities for coping with quantities of data. When they are forecasting the benefits of proposed HRD programs, decision makers are challenged by the overwhelming availability of so-called soft data. Soft data, which are generally not highly valued by decision makers, tends to have the following characteristics:

- Difficult to measure or quantify directly
- Difficult to assign dollar values to
- Based on subjective criteria
- Less credible as performance measures than hard data
- Usually behaviorally oriented

Conversely, although they can be more difficult to obtain, hard data are highly valued by decision makers because they appear to be accurate and precise. Hard data have the following characteristics:

- Easy to measure, quantitative
- Relatively easy to assign dollar values to

- Based on objective criteria
- Often already being used as measures of organizational performance
- Credible in the eyes of management

The importance of using hard data for forecasting purposes becomes obvious when one reviews the various levels at which evaluation takes place and the type of data upon which decision makers willingly stake their program decisions—and their reputations. There are three do-mains of results assessment—performance, learning, and perceptions (Swanson and Holton, 1999). Performance results focus on measures of mission-related outputs in the form of goods and services produced and the financial assessment of those outputs, including what it costs to pro-duce them.

The financial assessment model presented here can be used to assess the monetary benefits of HRD programs before, during, and after im-plementation. Following chapters explain how the model addresses these hard data issues and how the assessor can simply and systemati-cally work through a prescribed process to identify the expected perfor-mance value, costs, and benefits associated with each HRD program option.

A New View of HRD's Role

The economics of HRD are reflected in profit, strategy, and forecasting. I shall briefly examine each of these areas.

Profit. The old saying that business is in the business of making money reflects a fundamental value that HRD people must accept and support. If the HRD department cannot contribute to returns on investment, management must then try to minimize the costs associated with HRD activities. Thus, the HRD professional should either be tuned into the business of making money or be prepared to keep expenses to an abso-lute minimum.

Strategy. Many articles and books have been written and many speeches have been given about developing business strategy. The strategic plan-ning models that are generally available to management typically cover aspects of the organization's mission strategy and human resources, as well as the societal context in which the organization operates, including the economic, political, and cultural forces that impinge on it (Tichy, 1982). Understanding organizations and the context in which they must operate represents a new role for HRD people. Further, such matters are complex. Gearing up to support the business strategy means becoming increasingly cognizant of the economic factors that are involved in making strategic decisions. Being performance-based is the minimal requirement for HRD to be strategic (Torraco and Swanson, 1995).

Forecasting.   Tea leaves and crystal balls too often come to mind upon hearing the term *forecaster*. The best forecasters are those with good data. The most effective forecasters make timely forecasts. Right here, however, is where the greatest forecasting difficulty enters the picture. In general, forecasts are made at a point in time when decision makers do not have all the necessary data. Furthermore, obtaining the needed data almost precludes delivering a timely forecast. Risk taking is an essential element in melding available HRD data into the business timetable. Using an effective HRD financial forecasting model and method can increase one's confidence in the data and thus provide an element of security for the forecaster.

Conclusion

This chapter made a case for the economic analysis of HRD activities and for assessing the financial benefits of HRD. In doing so, I have presented the myths that stand in the way, the important relationships between performance requirement and financial benefit, and the basic financial concepts dictating a new organizational role for HRD.

The three components of the financial assessment model have been presented—performance value, cost, and benefit. The next step is to learn how to use the method and how to apply it. The three components of the model supply the organizers for Chapters 4, 5, and 6. Most authors on the economics of HRD have approached the subject from the cost perspective first (Head, 1993; Kearsley, 1982). They have then discussed the financial value of HRD in a few short paragraphs or dismissed it as being impossible to derive. That is not the case.

3

Process of Assessing Financial Benefits

Assessing financial benefits of human resource development (HRD) interventions is quite easy once you have mastered the specific techniques. The purpose of this chapter is to overview the *general process* of assessing financial benefits and to illustrate the assessment options through a simple case example. Thus, this chapter is a conceptual orientation to the process of assessing financial benefits of HRD (or any other intervention that purports to improve performance). Later chapters are dedicated to the specific techniques required of each of the three major components of the model (performance value, cost, and benefit) and to forecasted, actual, and approximate financial benefit assessment cases.

Methods for Assessing Financial Benefits

In Chapter 2 the basic financial assessment model was presented:

Performance Value (performance value resulting from HRD intervention)
- Cost   (cost of the HRD intervention)
Benefit   (benefit is the performance value minus the cost)

In later chapters you will see worksheets for each of the three components of the model. Now is *not* the time to figure out how to fill them out, just that the worksheets exist and that you will ultimately be able to fill them out properly.

A framework for assessing financial benefits was presented in Chapter 1 (see Figure 1.2). The framework identified three perspectives on assessing the financial benefits of HRD interventions:

- What is the *forecasted financial benefit* resulting from an HRD intervention? (Before-the-fact assessment based on estimated financial data.)
- What is the *actual financial benefit* resulting from an HRD intervention? (During-the-process assessment based on actual financial data.)
- What is the *approximate financial benefit* resulting from an HRD intervention? (After-the-fact assessment based on approximated financial data.)

These perspectives offer three financial benefit assessment strategies. Each relies on the same general method of getting to the performance value, cost, and benefit. A case example called "Tram Ride" will be introduced and then each of three financial benefit assessment methods will be applied and discussed in context of the Tram Ride case. The Tram Ride case is being used to build a conceptual understanding of the three financial benefit assessment methods. Later chapters in the book provide the how-to-do-it details.

Tram Ride Case

You are the HRD coordinator for the city zoo. The zoo's board of directors would like to make better use of the zoo's valuable volunteers by having them conduct tram tours on weekends. The board wants ten trained volunteers, each of whom would lead two tram tours per weekend. The net income from each tour is $40. No volunteers have previously been entrusted with this job, and you must now decide between what you believe are reasonable HRD program options. Would it be economically more beneficial to the zoo to train the volunteers by having them learn about the tram tours from experienced staff on the job or would it be more beneficial to have them use a self-instructional package?

The first option, on-the-job training, consists of trainees simply riding along with experienced operators until they are fully trained. It requires four hours of unstructured training time spread over two weekends for each trainee-volunteer. These trainee-volunteers will perform no tours on their own during the two-week training period. The second option, a self-instructional package, consists of a specially prepared map, a script, and an operation manual, which each of the volunteers will study for three to four hours as their first weekend commitment to their new volunteer job and they will be fully trained at the end of the first week. The trainee-volunteers who participate in this HRD program will conduct two tram tours (on their own) during the second week.

It is not the point of this case to argue whether these two options are the best or if they will actually do the job. Please assume that at the end of either program, each participating volunteer will be fully trained and able to conduct tram tours on his or her own.

For the purpose of illustration, all three methods (actual, forecasted, and approximate) will be discussed and the financial numbers will be kept the same throughout. The numbers will be as follows for all three assessment methods. And the self-instruction package will be determined to be the best option in terms of financial data.

	On-the-Job Training	Self-Instructional Training Packet
Performance Value	$0	$800
-Cost	- 0	- $300
Benefit	0	$500

Forecasting Financial Benefit Method

The *forecasting* method (Swanson and Gradous, 1988; Swanson, 1992) is one of the three methods being presented for assessing financial benefits of HRD. It is the "before-the-fact" method—before implementation. Financial forecasting is proactive and a part of the HRD up-front analysis and proposing phases. This method helps HRD professionals speak to decisionmakers about the forecasted estimate of the effects of an intervention on system performance and the financial consequences. Forecasts can be in the context of a particular HRD intervention or the relative financial benefits between intervention options. Forecasting financial benefits helps HRD professionals to influence organization investment decisions early on and helps HRD to be viewed as a business partner, proactive, and strategic.

Performance Value. From the case description it is clear that a completed tram tour is the appropriate unit of performance and that the two HRD program options for volunteer tram operators are on-the-job training and a self-instructional package. In this example, the zoo tram can be viewed as a "business" within a business in that it is a fairly self-contained system with zoo visitors paying an extra charge to ride the tram.

Furthermore, the goal of both HRD intervention options is the same—being able to conduct two tram tours per weekend. The average income for each tram ride is known to be $40. The city zoo has been running tram rides for several years and although they have this financial information, it is not generally known. It was obtained from the zoo's financial manager, who keeps records of income from various zoo operations.

A tram ride performance-time graph helps visualize the forecasting situation. The unit of performance and the performance goal is on the vertical axis—two tram rides per weekend for each of the trained volunteers. The horizontal time axis illustrates the fact that the self-instruction package gets volunteers to learn what they need to know in one week and that they are then able to conduct tram rides the second week. In comparison, on-the-job training requires two weekends riding along with an expert tram operator and on the third weekend they are ready to perform.

Another factor to keep in mind is the number of individual performers, groups, or systems involved. For the Tram Ride a total of ten volunteers will participate in the development program. Thus, individual performer gains need to be multiplied by ten.

The performance time graph illustrates the fact that all trainee-volunteers (in this case example) begin the program with zero tram expertise (zero performance). None have been exposed to the tram ride job before this occasion. Neither program option results in trainee-produced performance during their development periods. Note that an expert driver is operating the tram as the trainee-volunteer rides along. Every tram ride performed during the on-the-job training program is credited to

Program _____ Analyst _____ Date _____

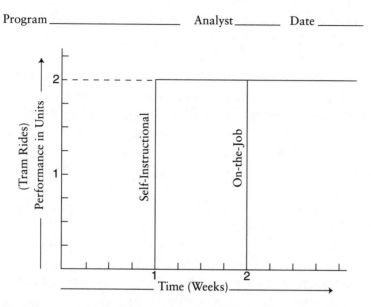

FIGURE 3.1   Tram Ride Time-Performance Graph

the skilled operator, not the trainee-volunteer. There is no added performance value in having the trainee along, and, in this situation (unlike most other HRD situations) there is no anticipated reduction in the performance of the skilled operator.

The unstructured on-the-job training option has a two-week development period during which no trainees conduct tram tours. The self-instructional package option has a one-week development period during which no volunteers conduct tram tours. These times to competence are judgments made by the HRD professional based on the complexity of the subject matter to be mastered and, in this tram case, the logistics of getting trainees and expert operators together for the on-the-job option. On-the-job training was estimated to take two weeks and the self-instructional package was to take one week. The longest development period between the two options is two weeks, and lists the units of performance during that time for both options. In this case, the self-instructional package volunteers conduct two tours during the two-week assessment period. The on-the-job volunteers conduct zero tours during the two-week assessment period.

Two tours per volunteer at $40 each times ten volunteers would add up to $800. This is the forecasted total performance value for the self-instructional package option during the two-week assessment period. There is a forecast of zero tours and $0 performance value for the on-the-job training program during the two-week development period.

Cost.   Forecasting the direct financial cost of HRD interventions requires a cost template that is backed up with experience or some price-data gathering. All HRD departments should have a defined process (such as analyze, propose, create, implement, assess; analyze, design, develop, implement, evaluate; and so on) and steps within the process phases. This process breakdown constitutes the cost categories. For the Tram Ride case, adding up the forecasted component costs within the cost categories for the self-instructional package resulted in a cost of $300. In comparison, there are no direct intervention costs for the unstructured on-the-job training option.

Benefit.   Forecasting the financial benefits is a simple subtraction problem. The forecasted performance value minus the forecasted cost results in the forecasted financial benefit. The $800 forecasted two-week period performance gain from the self-instructional program minus the $300 forecasted cost of the program yields a forecasted $500 benefit for the two-week period. The no-cost unstructured on-the-job option forecasted no direct cost and no performance value during the same two-week assessment period. Please note, however, that this case involves very short-range thinking—two weeks. If the zoo is open fifty weeks of the year and if the volunteers conduct twenty tours per weekend at $40 each, the net performance value for the year for *each option* would be close to $40,000. The only forecasted bad decision in this case would be not to recruit, develop, and use the volunteers.

Actual Financial Benefit Method

The method of assessing *actual financial* benefits of HRD (Swanson and Sawzin, 1975; Swanson, 1999) is the second of the three methods being presented. It is the "during-the-process" method—during the HRD process. Assessing the actual benefits is a deliberate and planned part of the full and ongoing HRD process. The method tracks the actual data as the HRD process unfolds. If doughnuts and coffee are provided at the implementation phase, the bill for the coffee and doughnuts is paid and recorded. The same three components of the financial assessment model come into consideration when determining actual financial benefits: *performance value* resulting from an intervention, the *cost* of the intervention, and the *financial benefit*, determined by subtracting cost from performance value.

Cost. Actual costs are the easiest financial numbers to track in any organization. Almost all organizations have cost accounting systems that work automatically. Therefore, the important thing to do is to match up cost categories with HRD process phases and steps regularly followed and then accurately capture the actual expenditures. The conceptual thinking here is identical to the cost thinking used with the forecasting method. Instead of estimating what the costs will be, actual expenditures are recorded and tallied after the fact or in an ongoing process.

If the HRD department asked an external consultant for a project bid, they likely would submit the bottom-line cost without a breakdown. For the city zoo example, here are the actual expenditures for the two options (and the third option of an invoice submitted by an external consultant for taking the self-instructional packet option):

HRD Process Phases	On-the-Job Training Costs	Self-Instructional Packet Cost	External Consultant Packet Cost
analyze	0	200	-----
propose	0	20	-----
create	0	220	-----
implement	0	20	-----
assess	0	40	------
Totals	$0	$300	$300

Performance Value.   The actual performance value is a matter of measuring the actual units of performance attributable to the HRD intervention. Following the earlier advice, this would mean mission-related outputs in the form of goods or services produced would be measured—a completed tram ride in this case. In the Tram Ride example, if everything went as forecasted, the actual units of performance attributable to the HRD intervention would match the up-front forecast. Since the city zoo keeps track of tram rides, the income per ride, and the driver of each tram ride, the actual number of rides and the actual ride income would be used. The tram performance log looks like this:

Tram Volunteer	Ride	Income
Sara Jones	10/09 am	$44
Sara Jones	10/09 pm	$38
William James	10/09 am	$36
William James	10/09 pm	$42

Benefit.   Determining the *actual financial* benefit continues to be the easy step in assessing financial benefits. It is simply a matter of subtracting the *actual* costs from the *actual* performance value for the *actual* financial benefit. In the Tram Ride case, this would be done for each option: For on-the-job training it is $0 − $0 = $0 and for the self-instructional package it is $800 − $300 = $500.

This is the time when HRD professionals report to decision makers the *actual* financial benefits resulting from an intervention implemented in their organization on system performance and its financial consequences. *Actual* financial benefits are the source of ultimate financial credibility of HRD in its host organization. It is from a track record of such assessments that financial generalizations about HRD emerge and general support is solidified.

Approximated Financial Benefit Method

The method of assessing *approximated* financial benefits of HRD (Swanson and Mattson, 1997; Mattson, 1998b) is the third method being presented. It is the "after-the-fact" method—after implementation of the HRD intervention. Assessing the approximated benefits is not part of the ongoing HRD process. The method is invoked following the implementation of a program—ex post facto. The approximated financial benefit method goes back to retrieve data and create relevant data after the fact.

Although this methodology differs from the *forecasted* and *actual* methods, the same three components of the financial assessment model come into consideration: performance value resulting from an intervention, the cost of the intervention, and the subtraction of the cost from the performance value to determine the benefit.

Cost.   Approximating the direct financial cost of HRD interventions requires a cost template just like the one used for the *forecasted* and *actual* methods. In that the intervention has already been implemented, the degree that the costs can been tracked by the organization's formal accounting system will vary from situation to situation. In some organizations you can go to the "expenditure" ledger and find it all to the point that it matches the actual—the records you would keep as the expenditures were made.

For the Tram Ride case it would be a matter of resurrecting the records of money spent and identifying those that are clearly Tram Ride expenditures. Where it is not clear, using the cost category template and ongoing HRD norms related to expenses, reasonable approximate numbers should be inserted. It is important to code numbers as verified or approximated. Again—for the purpose of illustration in the Tram Ride case—adding up the *approximated* component costs within the cost categories for the self-instructional package resulted in a cost of $300. In comparison, there were no direct intervention costs for the unstructured on-the-job training option.

Performance Value.   The process of *approximating* the performance value for after-the-fact financial benefit assessment requires some adjustment in thinking. The biggest adjustment has to do with the fact that an up-front performance diagnosis was not conducted. This step in the HRD processes has been celebrated as the most important step in ensuring that an HRD intervention will have performance and financial impact. This diagnosis focuses on the desired performance outcome and clarifies it in everybody's mind. In using the approximated method there is an effort to raise some of these key elements to a conscious and logical level. Elsewhere this method has been referred to as the critical outcome technique (COT). Swanson and Mattson (1997) originally developed the method and it has been more fully developed by Mattson and various colleagues (Mattson, Quartana, and Swanson, 1998, 1999; Mattson, 2000). The COT process has five steps: outcome definition, outcome inquiry, outcome verification, outcome valuation, and outcome report. The first is to create or re-create why the intervention was implemented. The cleaner this effort the better the information to insert in the financial benefit assessment. In the Tram Ride case, what was the desired outcome of training those volunteers? It was so that they could conduct tram tours. Step two, ask the trained volunteers if they actually conducted any tram rides and to specify all of them. Step three, have somebody in a position of knowledge or authority confirm that the reported rides actually took place. Step four, have somebody with the knowledge or authority tell what income those particular rides produced or what an average ride produces.

Cost.   At this point, depending on the situation, you will most likely have good, verifiable performance value data that will most likely be incomplete. For example, two volunteers dropped out and yet their training costs exist. In the end, I call this *approximate* data. The cost data can most likely be tracked down using the zoo's standard accounting and record-keeping system. This data can be plugged into the standard cost assessment worksheet.

Benefit.   Determining the *approximated* financial benefit continues to be the easiet step in assessing financial benefits. It is simply a matter of subtracting the *approximate* costs from the *approximate* performance value for the *approximate* financial benefit. In the Tram Ride case, this would be done for each option: For on-the-job training it is $0 − $0 = $0 and for the self-instructional package it is $800 − $300 = $500.

At this point HRD professionals put together reports on *approximate* financial benefits of an intervention. It is critical that the unit(s) of performance are specified and the self-report results attributed to the intervention by the participant are verified by another responsible person.

Conclusion

The purpose of this chapter was to overview the *general process* of assessing financial benefits and to illustrate the assessment options through a simple Tram Ride case example. This chapter is a conceptual orientation to the process of assessing financial benefits of HRD in terms of forecasted, actual, and approximated data.

Calculating the Performance Value

4

Performance is the key to assessing the financial benefits of HRD. All work in organizations should be aimed at meeting performance goals, such as contributing to profit, increasing product or service quality, or remaining in the good graces of regulators. Performance goals are essential to the long-term viability of organizations and to the jobs they sustain. Responsible HRD interventions influence positive changes related to specific performance goals and are measured in dollars and cents. This chapter provides the information you will need to determine the value of such performance.

Remember, what gets measured gets done (Peters, 1987) and "everything important in business and industry is evaluated" (Swanson, 1989, 1). If HRD professionals don't measure their successes, others will do the measuring for them. The methods of measuring that other people use tend to underestimate HRD's real contributions. By assessing financial benefits, HRD professionals can determine and communicate their contributions to the organization—just as Greg Hill recently learned to do.

Performance Opportunity

Greg Hill walked with confidence into the regular Friday morning meeting of his senior management team. He was well prepared. A few hours of examining production reports and scrap records had yielded the figures he sought. Now, here he was, ready to show that the new job guides his department had prepared for the operators of the B-14 machines had already returned an astonishing $12 for every $1 invested in them. Although the other members of the group acknowledged the good results of the B-14 job guide program, Greg remembered how hard he had fought to hire an expensive HRD consultant to help write the job guides. Without a doubt, Sue Parker was worth more than her large consulting fee. By making a careful work analysis and exercising her excellent writing skills, she had created a number of precise and effective job guides. Then, too, she had used her skill in working with people to ensure that the new guides would be well received by the operators. For the last eight months, the operators have checked their job guides *before* adjusting their machines for each new job lot—instead of *after* making a short run of unacceptable pieces. Greg's calculations of the worth of these new work behaviors to the organization were as follows:

Performance Value	
(increased product + decreased scrap)	$169,700
Cost of B-14 Job Guide Program	−$18,000
Benefit	$151,700

Talking Management's Language

Greg Hill has learned how to communicate in the language of the senior management team, and all HRD professionals have a similar opportunity. In the past, many of them have talked easily and well about such issues as keeping valued customers and aligning reward systems with desired performances. Those are important goals. But these HRD professionals have failed to talk about programs in the language that top management understands best—dollars and cents.

The challenge is to convert HRD jargon into the language that is most easily understood by management, the language of financial gains and benefits. Once this challenge is met, HRD professionals will be prepared to answer management's question, "What does HRD really contribute to the company?" The conceptual starting point in answering this question is with the HRD worldview model that was presented in Figure 1.1. With this picture in mind, the following simple but essential questions need to be answered in context of the particular HRD intervention being financially assessed:

1. Name of the organization (total system or stand-alone subsystem):

_____

2. Mission of the host "organization" [no. 1 above]:

_____

3. If the "framed" system being assessed is not no. 1 above, identify and name one below:

___ Subsystem?   _____

___ Work process?   _____

___ Work group?   _____

___ Job?   _____

4. Identify and name the mission-related unit of output performance being impacted through the HRD intervention [for no. 3]:

___ Goods produced?   _____

___ Services produced?   _____

Knowing the unit of mission-related output is still not enough to talk about financial benefits, as there is a need to know how to calculate the *value of performance.* Performance gains, whether expressed in terms of quantity, timeliness, or quality features of products and services, generally represent money in the bank.

It is a challenge to establish the performance value of work, but with a little thought and careful investigation the value of any performance in any organization can be calculated. That is, *if the HRD intervention contributes to the performance goals of the company, it can be valued in dollars and cents.* Whenever HRD programs are directed toward reaching the organization's performance goals by accomplishing outputs that are valued in dollars and cents, the odds are greatly increased that HRD will be taken seriously in that organization.

An Approach to Performance Value Analysis

To calculate the value of improved performance, gather four pieces of information:

- *Unit of performance.* Some clearly definable unit of work or system performance is always present in any work system or job role. If it cannot be identified, perhaps the HRD program is not worth considering.
- *Performance levels.* Both the existing level of performance and the target level of performance to be reached in a designated period of time must be determined.
- *Value of each unit.* Each defined unit of performance must be valued in dollars and cents.
- *Performance value.* Performance value is obtained by multiplying the value of one unit of performance times the total number of units that can be attributed to the HRD program.

The method for determining each piece of information on the performance value worksheet will be explained later in this chapter. For now, the following discussion helps to understand how each piece of information is used in performance value analysis.

What Are Units of Performance?   A decision must be made about what the *unit* of expected performance is. The objective is to relate this unit directly to the original performance needs assessment and to the work performance that will result from the HRD program. For example, units expected to result from the HRD program could be retail sales, insurance forms processed, machines maintained, employees counseled, or customers retained.

When attempts are made to determine the unit of performance, the issue of separating wants from needs becomes important and this is why the diagnosing performance aspect of the up-front analysis phase is so important (for a detailed presentation of the analysis phase see Swanson, 1996). For example, the chief executive officer may demand that he see less paper flow at headquarters. Yes, some measurable unit of paper flow could then be defined. But too much paper flow is probably only a symptom of the real problem. A good performance diagnosis in this instance would have revealed that the way the organization is currently structured has led to unclear lines of responsibility and decisionmaking authority, which in turn has caused a spate of excessive and inefficient communications about relatively unimportant matters. Because paper flow is just a symptom of the real problem, it should *not* be the unit of work performance to be improved by the HRD program. The unit of performance to be measured might better be the time period between a business proposal being made and formal action being taken—the timeliness of critical decisions in the organization.

What Is the Performance Level? Performance level is the amount of something accomplished. Calculating the performance value often requires determining the beginning performance level as well as the performance level after an intervention. The current performance level is the amount of performance accomplished at the beginning of the HRD program. The target performance level is the amount of performance expected at the end of the HRD program or at some designated later time.

For example, an HRD program to institute a new reward system in a large financial organization was expected to decrease the number of managers who left the firm. To avoid working the performance value calculations in negative numbers, the HRD consultant reviewed the company's records and discovered that 180 managers had been retained each year. He predicted that as a result of implementing his HRD program, 186 managers would be retained in the coming year. In this example, the beginning performance level is 180 and the target level, or performance goal, is 186. The forecasted performance goal of 6 additional retained managers represents value to the organization. Accurately, *forecasting* performance levels requires analysis skills and confidence in the quality of HRD programs before the intervention. Determining the *actual* retention is a matter of following the data during the intervention, and *estimating* the performance after the fact will most likely produce the same data as the actual performance. This is because the organization's database will likely stay intact and be available at the later time.

Even small gains in performance are worth a great deal when they are multiplied over time or for many workers. For example, suppose that an organization employs about 200 managers and about 10 percent of them leave every year. In positive terms, the organization has a 90 percent retention rate. A performance diagnosis clearly identifies that ongoing, inexpert supervisory behavior is causing managerial resentment and turnover. The HRD department believes it can partly remedy this situation. A promise to increase the proportion of managers retained to 100 percent would be considered quite unrealistic. No organization can expect to totally satisfy all its employees. Furthermore, good managers may be offered outside job opportunities that the organization is unwilling to match. A conservative performance goal, one that is reachable given the situation and the resources dedicated to the task, will be set. In this situation, promising a 93 percent retention rate for managers was realistic. Three percent, or six managers, may seem like a small gain in performance, but when this number is multiplied by the dollar value of one retained manager, the performance value gain is significant. Performance goals, besides being accurate, must be realistic, obtainable, and significant.

What Is the Value of a Performance Unit?   The financial *value* of one unit of performance must also be determined. Each unit of performance, whether it is a lowered level of employee turnover or a higher level of products produced, is worth something to the organization. Accountants or other fiscal managers can generally assist in estimating this value by checking company records. In Acme Company, for example, the current finished inventory of 6,000 widgets is carried on the books at $12,000. At this rate, one widget—one performance unit—is worth $2. The accountant agrees that this is a conservative valuation.

In a similar vein, the manager of the claims department will probably know the value of processing additional insurance forms. Let's say that 18,000 forms are processed each week by forty-five people at a cost of $45,000. The company goal is to achieve this performance with forty people—a savings of $5,000 per week. In consultation with department managers, the HRD manager develops a new work design for the claims-processing task. This new work design makes the expected performance level possible. The performance value of achieving this goal is 28 cents per form, $5,040 per week, or about $131,000 over the next twenty-six weeks. The company reaps the rewards of the performance gain, and the HRD department earns the respect of management.

Returning to the previous example on managerial turnover, it is usually fairly easy for a company to place a dollar value on employee turnover. In fact, most organizations know what it costs to replace an employee at any level in the organization. Replacing good employees who leave is usually a very costly matter. Instituting a new supervisory organization development and training program to eliminate even a small portion of this turnover expense can represent a significant financial gain for the organization.

What Is the Performance Value? Performance value is the financial worth of the number of performance units that result from an HRD program. The performance value of an HRD program is calculated by multiplying the total number of units expected to result from the program times the dollar value of one unit.

To illustrate this, look again at the turnover case. The HRD manager estimated that six additional managers per year would be retained as a result of the HRD program. Six managers times the organization's average turnover expense of $75,000 per manager is a performance value of $450,000. In this case, both the number of *units* (six) and the financial *value* of each unit ($75,000) were conservative estimates.

This brief discussion of the four pieces of information needed for valuing performance—unit, performance levels, unit value, and performance value—has set the stage for an in-depth look at the process of assessing the performance value.

Computing the Performance Value

As noted earlier, the basic financial assessment model has three elements—performance value, cost, and benefit. Of the three, determining the performance value requires the most extensive calculations. Even so, *the method is orderly, not very complex, and one that HRD people have used successfully time and time again.* The earlier description of the elements required to conduct the assessment has revealed a small portion of the method for assessing the value of performance. To become competent at assessing financial benefits, more knowledge and additional tools are required. The remainder of this chapter covers the process for generating financial data and provides a worksheet for assessing the *performance values* expected to result from proposed HRD programs. In a similar way, the following chapters will cover program *costs* and program *benefits*.

When engaged in the assessment process, it is important to keep two perspectives in mind. One perspective is that of the *venture capitalist,* the other, that of the *accountant.* The proper perspective is like that of the venture capitalist, who is trying to make the best investment decision, not trying to figure the money to the penny. The business investor tries to estimate the gains from a particular course of action, relies on common sense, and is willing to take risks. Venture capitalists do not worry unnecessarily about every detail. Their main activity is big-picture planning. Assessing financial benefits of HRD programs is the same sort of big-picture activity.

The performance value worksheet (Figure 4.1) assists in keeping the big-picture thinking. The worksheet also acts as a guide through the process. The worksheet asks the questions that need to be answered. The form provides space to record responses. The worksheet assumes that you understand the financial assessment process. It uses the four pieces of information already talked about. Fortunately, the completed worksheet can be easily interpreted by decision makers who have little or no knowledge of the process you used to get your figures. The remainder of this chapter is dedicated to a more detailed description of the logic to use in filling out each line of the worksheet. At first glance, the worksheet may appear somewhat formidable. The responses to items *a* through *g* provide all the information needed to determine the performance value expected to result from an HRD program.

When beginning, be sure to record the HRD program or intervention name, your name, and the date in the worksheet heading. Don't fail to perform this step because it will probably be needed later. The next information called for on the worksheet heading is the names of all the HRD program options being considered. Here are two pieces of advice as you explore the important question about HRD program options.

- Connect your HRD program to the performance goal that was identified during the performance needs assessment.
- Consider the full range of HRD options with which to address the performance goal before choosing two to four of the most reasonable ones.

Program/Intervention _____ Analyst _____ Date _____

	Option name: 1_____	2_____
Data required for calculations:		
(a) What unit of performance are you measuring?	_____ unit name	_____ unit name
(b) What is the performance goal per worker/group/system at the end of your HRD program?	___ ___ / ___ no. units / time	___ ___ / ___ no. units / time
(c) What is the performance per worker/group/system at the beginning of the HRD program?	___ ___ / ___ no. units / time	___ ___ / ___ no. units / time
(d) What dollar value is assigned to each performance unit?	$_____/unit	$_____/unit
(e) What is the development time required to reach the expected performance level?	___ ___ no. time	___ ___ no. time
(f) What is the assessment period? (Enter the longest time (e) of all options being considered.)	___ ___ no. time	___ ___ no. time
(g) How many workers/groups/systems will participate in your HRD program?	_____ no. workers/groups/ systems	_____ no. workers/groups/ systems
Calculations to determine net performance value:		
(h) Useable units workers/groups/systems produce during the HRD program? If no, enter -0-. If yes, enter known performance rate or calculate average performance rate [(b + c)/2]	___ ___ no. units	___ ___ no. units
(i) What are the total units per worker/group/system produced during the development time? (h x e)	_____ no. of units	_____ no. of units
(j) How many units produced per worker/work group/system during the assessment period? {[(f − e) x b] + i}	_____ no. of units	_____ no. of units
(k) What is the value of the worker's/group's/system's performance during the assessment period? (j x d)	$ _____	$ _____
(l) What is the performance value gain per worker/group/system? [k − (c x d x f)]	$ _____	$ _____
(m) What is the total performance value gain for all workers/groups/systems? (l x g)	$ _____ (Option 1)	$ _____ (Option 2)

Note that performance units and time units for all options <u>must remain consistent</u> throughout the assessment.

FIGURE 4.1   Performance Value Worksheet

Performance diagnoses are critical to implementing responsible HRD programs. These assessments help in identifying the basic performance requirements on which business goals depend. Even given an excellent performance diagnosis, one that explores performance levels and performance variables, HRD managers sometimes use the wrong criteria to select HRD programs. They do this because of the biases of top managers, their own prior experience with available HRD programs, or an infatuation with certain HRD program delivery methods. But each of these reasons should remain secondary to the main question, whether the program is capable of producing the desired performance.

Assessing the financial benefits of an HRD program connects the performance diagnosis to the HRD intervention in a dramatic fashion. The performance requirement, the intervention to meet that requirement, and the dollar value of the resulting performance ought to be clearly related. When the performance requirement and the HRD intervention cannot be clearly and directly connected and when no dollar value can be attached to the performance goal, the HRD manager should reconsider the results of the performance goal, the possible HRD program options, or the appropriateness of HRD as a means to achieve the identified performance goal. When HRD managers deliberately raise such questions as they fill in the performance value worksheet, the odds of achieving harmony among goals, interventions, and performance results are increased. Thus, as part of the decisionmaking process, HRD managers, designers, and program providers need to ask themselves if they truly believe that their HRD programs will result in the specified performance goal and what evidence or logic they have to back up their claims.

To guard against routine habits of thinking, which will often be counterproductive in finding the best HRD solutions, divergent thinking is important. For instance, one company that I worked with was so accustomed to purchasing management training from external providers and designing its own technical training that it failed to ask external providers to bid on technical training projects. On one occasion I nudged the HRD manager into procuring an external bid for a technical training program. She was shocked to discover that the external provider was willing to produce and deliver a program comparable to the proposed in-house program at an earlier date and at 70 percent of the cost.

The manager realized that she had probably ignored many excellent program alternatives in the past.

Figure 4.2 is a useful map for thinking about a range of structured HRD options. The source axis reminds us to consider using both internal and external providers. The type axis reminds us to consider a variety of custom-made and off-the-shelf programs. Any proposed HRD program option will fall either into a single cell or into some combination of the cells. Program C illustrates an off-the-shelf program that was customized by a team of internal and external HRD personnel to meet the needs and style of the organization and was then delivered by internal HRD personnel.

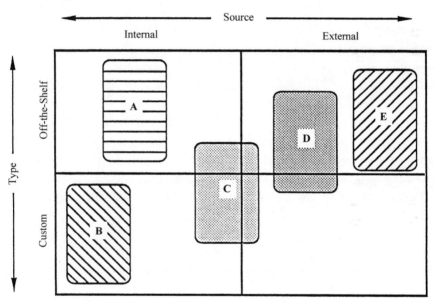

FIGURE 4.2   HRD Program Options

Another important role of assessment is to compare structured HRD program options to the existing unsatisfactory situation. Existing unsatisfactory situations can result from both formal (structured) or informal (unstructured) HRD programs. Remember, there is no such thing as no HRD. The existing HRD program may be unconscious, unplanned, unsystematic, and ineffective—in a word, unstructured. Even so, such unstructured HRD programs are in place. They are usually assigned no direct costs and they generally bring unknown financial consequences to the organization. If an unstructured program or an unsatisfactorily structured program is already in place in your organization, it cannot help but make the assessment of the benefits from responsible structured HRD program options look good. Certainly, you should show the current unsatisfactory condition as one of your program options.

Performance Description

The first major item on the performance value worksheet (Figure 4.1) is to describe the performance expected to or actually resulting from the HRD program (item *a*). The skilled assessor may be able to answer this question straight out, but a less experienced assessor will first need to answer a series of subquestions that begin with describing the performance expected to result from the program, exploring the dimensions of that performance, and establishing levels of performance within those dimensions. After this preparatory step, the assessor will then decide on the unit of performance (item a) to use in determining the performance value of the HRD program. In responding to these subquestions, the analyst will produce the information for the following worksheet items (Figure 4.1):

(a) What unit of performance are you measuring?
(b) What is the performance goal per worker/group/system at the end of the HRD program?
(c) What is the performance per worker/group/system at the beginning of the HRD program (mission-related goals or services

The subquestions leading to worksheet items *a*, *b*, and *c* are as follows:
(*a*) *What unit of performance are you measuring?*

- What is your best description of the performance resulting from the HRD program (mission-related goods or services)?
- Is there a measure of time associated with the performance? If yes, what is it?

- Is there a measure of quantity associated with the performance? If yes, what is it?
- Is there a measure of quality associated with the performance? If yes, what is it?

(b)   *What is the performance goal per worker/group/system at the end of the HRD program?*

- What is the performance measure goal in terms of mission-related goods or services produced?
- Are performance measures (time, quantity, quality features) already being kept by the organization?
- Is it reasonable to measure this performance (time, quantity, quality features) in the organization?

(c)   *What is the performance per worker/group/system at the beginning of the HRD program?*

- Unit of Performance: _____
- Time, Quantity, and Quantity Features: _____
- Measure: _____

What reasonable alternatives will be considered for the measure of performance?

- Unit of Performance: _____
- Time, Quantity, and Quantity Features: _____
- Measure: _____

What is your final decision about the measure of work performance you will measure and how it will be assessed?

Explanation of the Subquestions

The first subquestion asks for an *initial* statement about the performance that will result from the HRD program. This answer is best derived from the performance diagnosis. Depending on the situation, the answer could specify a clear unit of performance that has value to the organization, or the answer could still be fuzzy and in need of further clarification. For example, a performance diagnosis in one large organization pointed to an excess number of lengthy and inefficient meetings. The initial work performance goal was described as "less time spent in meetings." A planned HRD program with the objective of improving skills in selecting attendees for the meetings was considered. In their performance needs assessment, however, the analysts missed the critical point that the performance goal of managers in this organization is neither attending meetings nor running shorter meetings. If this were so, participating managers, upon completion of the HRD program, would know how to run efficient meetings and they could then comfortably return to their jobs. The expected performance in this case probably had something to do with the *timeliness* of managerial decisions, the *quantity* of work performed back on the job with the time gained from shorter meetings, or the need for significant improvement in the *quality features* of the decisions made during the meetings. To help sort out these tough questions about work performance, the subquestions probe further.

In exploring the exact nature of performance units, the assessor can look at three measurement dimensions:

- Time
- Quantity
- Quality features

Performance units assessed in all three dimensions can ultimately be quantified. The HRD program should be aimed at measurable improvements of mission-related outputs in one or more of the measures.

Time here is defined as the measurable interval between two events or the period during which some activity occurs. In the workplace, performance is commonly measured in terms of time. Gains in performance time usually yield important financial consequences to the organization.

The situation at the drive-through window of a fast-food restaurant illustrates this point nicely. It was discovered that by moving the air-hose bell twenty feet ahead of the ordering point the order taker could be on call at the moment the vehicle driver stopped at the window to place an order. This change in the workplace reduced the time to process each order by several valuable seconds. In another situation, I observed an HRD program that resulted in a four-month reduction in the amount of time it took sales personnel to learn their jobs fully. In another instance, the new product design and setup teams learned to cut their design-to-production time in half—a highly valued outcome, given their organization's competitive race to the marketplace.

Quantity is a measure of the exact amount or number of products, services, or other outcomes that result from worker or group performances. Quantity units are relatively easy to define and monitor in the workplace. Examples of such quantity units are the numbers of patents approved, clients served, sundaes sold, and sales earned. All three of the performance dimensions must be quantified, but the "quantity" dimension is the only one that is restricted to counting the simple, usually observable, worker or group outputs.

Quality features are the characteristics of products or services that meet agreed-upon specifications. Some of the quality features of a product or service include design, procurement, manufacturing, marketing, sales, service, customer education, and ultimate disposition (Tribus, 1985). I know of a computer manufacturer that has a set of requirements in all these areas. The manufacturer's design specifications focus on such features as the size and capabilities of the computer. Its specifications for sales and customer education include such quality features as acceptable selling practices and a method for determining customer training needs. Because most companies compete with each other on the basis of meeting customer specifications, improvements in product or service quality features are worth dollars and cents to the company. Consequently, HRD interventions that enhance product or service quality features have value to their companies.

HRD interventions can be aimed at improving either *end-product* or *in-process* quality features. End-product quality features are characteristics of the final product or service. In the computer manufacturing example, an end-product quality feature would be an increase in the quality of the surface finish of the monitor, which would make it more attractive to both the distributor and the retail customer.

In-process features are characteristics that products or services have while they are being made. Organizations often determine in-process quality specifications that products and services must meet with the expectation that these, in turn, will lead to desired end-product quality features. For example, it is important to an airline that passengers feel a great deal of confidence when they fly on a commercial airline. Management expects pilots to follow prescribed preflight check-sheet procedures (in-process specifications) and to get to their destination safely (end-product specification). Common sense suggests that the forecaster should not always wait for an end-product measure to determine whether an in-process performance is valuable. If this were the case, pilots could neglect their in-process check sheets until a sufficient number of near-fatal or fatal accidents warranted a crackdown on their work performance.

As you can see, I have rather narrowly defined the dimensions of time, quantity, and quality features. Broader definitions would not be particularly useful for determining the units of work to use in forecasting the short-term financial benefits of HRD. For example, a forecaster could agonize unnecessarily over how to express the two dimensions of quantity and time. Time can be expressed in two ways: numbers of units produced in a set block of time or the time needed to produce each unit of performance. Thus, the performance goal could be to increase the *number* of widgets made or the *number* of counseling sessions conducted in an eight-hour day. Or the performance goal could be to decrease the *time* it takes to produce a widget or conduct a counseling session. In the drive-through window situation, the performance goal could be expressed as total number of sales during a period of time rather than as the time required for each sale.

In financial assessment, the performance value is directly related to the time, quantity, or quality features of the expected units of work performance. The calculation will focus on just one of these dimensions, but the HRD manager needs to consider all three to achieve excellent results. If the analyst at the performance diagnosis stage were to focus on a single dimension—time, quantity, or quality features—without being aware of their interrelatedness, the organizations would likely end up in trouble. I recall a bank where the customer service personnel were given incentive pay for the number of telephone calls they completed. Whenever the computers were not operating, the customer service people told each caller only that the computer was down. They then hung up the telephone, took the next call, and added to their in-centive pay. The needs of the customers were ignored. In this instance, an emphasis on quantity-only criteria led to a significant loss in important quality features.

For assessment purposes, time, quantity, or quality features must be chosen as the primary vehicle for valuing performance gains. At the same time, the HRD manager must remember to monitor the other two dimensions. Assessing the full range of work performance dimensions at the analysis phase ensures that the HRD intervention does not promote gains in one dimension at the expense of the other two.

To summarize the discussion of the measures of time, quantity, and quality features, I offer some examples of performance unit output:

Time (focus on the period during which something happens):

- Two minutes to process a fast-food order
- Forty manufacturing hours per generator housing
- Fifty minutes per service call

Quantity (focus on numbers of things):

- Twenty circuit boards per worker per eight-hour shift
- Five employees coached per week in team-building skills
- $110,000 new-car sales per month
- 999,999 out of 1,000,000 acceptance rate of .50-inch-diameter metal rings per thirty days of production

Quality Features (focus on attributes):

- A four-point or higher annual satisfaction rating for hotel accommodations and service
- Five customer courtesy steps taken on 100 percent of the monthly transactions
- Ninety-five percent acceptable (pass) fruity wine bouquet per forty-hour inspection period

All the dimensions cited are positive, and represent gains that can be stated in positive numbers. Although it is possible to work with negative numbers by citing absolute values, the HRD financial forecasting method requires positive values. For example, the forecaster can cite "fewer defects in a product" through its inverse, "gains in acceptable products."

Performance Levels

Thus far I have described two items on the performance value worksheet (Figure 4.1) by working through the subquestions:

(a) What unit of performance are you measuring?

(b) What is the performance goal per worker/group/system at the end of the HRD program?

Item *c* on the worksheet has to do with determining the beginning performance level in units of performance that are still being considered:

(c) What is the performance per worker/group/system at the beginning of the HRD program?

At this point all three features—time, quantity, and quality features—could still be under consideration as potential measures of performance. Here I raise a few questions about measurement and organizational record keeping. The answers will help to choose the most practical measure of the unit of performance for a specific HRD program.

If organizational records are already being kept on a unit of work that leads to the performance goal, this measure of work will obviously be much more attractive than one on which no records are being kept. Existing records provide a basis for comparison over time and eliminate the effort and expense of setting up a special measurement scheme. Existing records are usually seen as credible and not open to manipulation. Ideally, you will find an existing record of one of the units of performance that you have under consideration.

As a rule, organizations keep records of the work performances that are *critical* to the organization. If the proposed HRD program is truly focused on important performances, the odds are good that records are already being kept on the performance of the targeted individuals or system. Sources of useful records include departmental production and scrap records, accounting department figures, business plans and reports, and sales and service charts.

If appropriate records are not being kept, the next subquestion asks, Is it possible to collect and record the data? Without a system in place for keeping records of the performance, the assessor may need to propose one. If so, the overriding concern is that the record-keeping system be both valid and simple. For example, one assessor settled on the simple and direct measure of new memberships as the most important unit of performance. The organization's HRD and marketing departments were simultaneously engaged in programs designed to gain new members. A meeting of vice presidents to decide on the *relative performance value* of the two programs was the best available means for separating contributions of the individual programs. The decision by upper management was credible to everyone in the organization. The unit of performance— new members—was simple, valid, and useful.

Unit of Performance Decision

I have walked through the process for deciding the unit of performance and have looked at dimensions of work performance, checked out existing performance record-keeping systems in the organization, and cited the need for credibility.

At this point, a meaningful decision can be made about the unit of work performance that will be used to assess the financial benefit of the proposed HRD program. Ultimately, this decision is easy because answers to the subquestions have either confirmed or redirected your thinking. Perhaps only one or two of the three dimensions of performance units are left for consideration. The final choice should be based on practical concerns. Which HRD unit of performance option is

- Most clearly connected to the original need?
- Easiest to implement?

Thus, the harmony among performance goals, program, and results is once again tested and confirmed in this decision.

Value of Unit of Performance

With answers to items *a*, *b*, and *c* filled in on the performance value worksheet, finding the answer to item *d* is the next step:

(d) What dollar value is assigned to each performance unit?

This question, more than any other, intimidates assessors. But sitting at your desk and fretting over it will not lead you to the answer. Getting up and talking to non-HRD people is generally the only realistic means of acquiring the answer. People in your organization keep numbers on almost everything. Sometimes these numbers are unknown to the people who actually carry out the work activity in which you are interested. Sometimes they are known only to the people who are one or two tiers above the activity within the organization.

The HRD staff members of a manufacturing company were attempting to forecast the financial benefit of training workers to operate some new machining centers. They talked to the machinists, to the supervisors, and even to the department head to get a "good number" to use in their forecast. When nothing came up their inquiries, they asked me to come by for a short conference. I did so. After listening to their frustrations, I suggested that they call the vice president of manufacturing at home, as it was then 6:30 P.M. The vice president had authorized the purchase of the machining centers. Within seconds he informed the HRD director that the machining centers were expected to put out $635 of product per hour. There it was. The dollar value that had been used to make the purchasing decision could now be used to *forecast* the HRD decision. When doing an assessment of the *actual* financial benefit it would be a matter of recording *actual* production records.

Advice on assigning a dollar value to a unit of performance falls into two categories: source and method. As noted above, the source is usually outside the boundary of the HRD office and within the boundary of the financial decision makers for the business or for a particular part of the business. The information required may be on paper or it may be in someone's head. In either case, access to the information will be through non-HRD people. You will need to call, visit, and cajole department heads, accountants, and vice presidents of sales and marketing to get the information you need.

Two useful questions for locating the *sources* of the dollar value of each unit of performance include:

- Does someone in the organization already know this value?
- What manager or accountant would most likely know this value?

Once again, the closer the HRD program is connected to an important performance goal of the organization, the easier it will be to find good sources for the requisite financial information. Thus, the harmonious connection among need, program, and results is tested once again.

Obviously, you will not have to choose a method for placing a dollar value on a unit of performance if the organization has already done the job for you. Regrettably, this will not always be the case. The value may be missing or it may be imbedded in the value of a larger unit of work that your program only partially addresses. In such a case, an intelligent estimate is required. Intelligent estimates hinge on two notions:

- *Estimating* the dollar value of each unit of performance is okay.
- The estimator must have *credibility or authority* in the organization.

Remember, however, that it is the venture capitalist's view of finances you are using, not the accountant's view. Estimates are acceptable. We use them all the time in making life decisions, and organizations use them for making very big decisions. Learn to feel comfortable with estimating the financial worth of units of performance. To become an effective assessor, you must rely on the help of appropriate people in your organization. Clearly, if you have access to the hard numbers, use them. If not, you must estimate them. Just be sure to consult with individuals who have credibility or authority in your organization. Trade and professional journals that report the standard dollar value of units of work performance are credible sources. If such published figures are applicable to your company, use them. Do not go it alone; rely on others.

For a close look at dollar valuing, we can review the situation with which Barb Johnson, director of HRD, was faced. Barb Johnson saw a serious communication problem in the manufacturing firm for which she worked. The problem had to do with the technical language that was used by teams of design engineers, prototype/setup people, and production workers—a language called *geometric tolerancing*. In Barb's company all kinds of awkward and counterproductive work behaviors occurred because the production workers did not understand the language of geometric tolerancing. The prototype/setup people knew a little of this language, and the design engineers knew a lot. The engineers in particular were using their know-how about geometric tolerancing to get their way. Even when the engineers were, in fact, wrong, the others could not communicate on the same ground.

Barb knew that a common understanding of the language of geometric tolerancing would get the teams back on track, which in this situation would mean significant reductions in the time it took to make compromise decisions between the three levels of manufacturing. The unit of performance that was expected to result from the HRD geometric tolerancing training, therefore, was a reduction in the number of days it took to achieve compromise manufacturing decisions and a corresponding gain in the number of days of productive work. Putting a value on the days of productive work that would be gained was the most difficult estimating problem that Barb had yet encountered. Here is how she proceeded: First, she identified key people in the firm who were versed in its productivity and work system. They knew time and materials costs and could discuss such matters as the flow of products within the organization. Second, she obtained available records of average times for design, redesign, and production. She also gathered information about scrap costs and the production rates associated with part types. Third, she met with the director of manufacturing and an accountant to obtain agreement on what they thought the financial consequences of protracted decisionmaking had been. (They identified engineering time spent on redesign and production losses during redesign period.) Fourth, she obtained agreement from the director of manufacturing that production rate was the most useful unit of performance *and* that it was a very conservative estimate of the true financial picture. Finally, she was able to get the same decision maker to place an estimated value of $18,500 for production per eight-hour day.

Johnson now had the necessary information to answer items a and d on the performance value worksheet. You, like Barb Johnson, will run into some seemingly difficult valuing situations. Always remember that you need to step outside of your office, that it is all right to make estimates, and that you should rely on others who have the credibility or authority to make decisions about unit performance values.

Time to Reach Performance Goal

An important task in comparing HRD program options is to answer worksheet item *e*, which asks about the development time it takes participants to get to the performance goal:

(e) What is the development time required to reach the expected performance level?

You will recall from Chapter 2 that time differences in reaching performance goals can result in costly losses or valuable gains in productivity. Figure 4.3 compares structured with unstructured HRD, a situation where the gains in valued performance are relatively assured. But when you undertake to estimate the time requirements, another gut-wrenching issue surfaces: Does each option have the capability of achieving the desired performance goal? That, however, is another problem and another book. For purposes of the present discussion, I assume that the answer for each option is yes.

Once the unit of performance has been established, the unit of time should be specified. Typical time units include hours, days, or weeks. It is wise to use whatever units of time your organization typically uses and always to keep the time units constant within the forecast. Only very unusual HRD programs would use time increments as small as minutes or as large as months. Sometimes HRD programs will have a short classroom session or retreat followed by one or more structured activities in the workplace. When follow-up activities are part of the HRD program, the forecaster will probably use weeks rather than hours as the preferred unit.

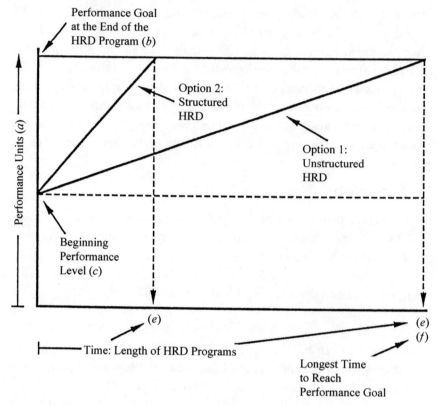

FIGURE 4.3   Time-Performance Graph Showing Data Sources

Selecting the unit of time is the easy part. The more difficult part is estimating the time it will take to achieve the desired performance goal for each HRD program option. Here are two bits of down-home advice:

• Call it as you see it.
• Move on.

Have you ever umpired a baseball game? Your first time is a funny experience. If you don't call the pitches, the players and fans will. You soon learn that the worst thing is to *not* call the pitches as they come at you. In some ways being an assessor is like being an umpire. You never know for sure, but you have seen pitches like that before, and so you call them.

Several of the HRD financial assessment tasks require you to "call them as you seem them" and to move on. Estimating the time to reach a goal is one of those tasks. The pressure you feel comes from the fact that your estimate must have credibility with the decision makers who will review your information.

If a program will be designed by someone else in the HRD department or by an outside provider, have that person make the time estimate. If there are too many political agendas in the work environment, have the manager make it. As in baseball, the official closest to the play calls it. The estimated time to reach the performance goal should be determined for each HRD program option under consideration and recorded in answer to item e of the worksheet (Figure 4.1).

Assessment Period

The assessment period for the financial assessment is the longest time of all the HRD program options being considered. Thus, the longest of the times entered as item *e* on the worksheet is the proper response to item *f* (Figure 4.1).[1]

(f) What is the assessment period?

(Enter the longest time *[e]* of all the options being considered.)

Getting this number is easy, but it is important to think about the reason for using the *longest time* as the assessment period. You have already been introduced to the idea that times to reach the work performance goal will vary. An HRD program option that brings people to the performance goal more rapidly should get credit for performance.

Unstructured HRD situations in which people develop slowly and at relatively low levels of performance must be valued on the same basis as other program options. If they are not, some decision makers will be inclined to wave their "we don't spend money on HRD" flags without ever realizing how much their unstructured HRD programs are costing their organization.

---

[1]There are instances when longer time frames are needed to assess results because of organizational data collection norms or data collection restrictions.

Participation

Item *g* of the worksheet (Figure 4.1) asks:

(g) *How many workers/groups/systems will participate in the HRD program?*

The number of participants is usually easy to establish and should already be known from the performance needs assessment. However, the number derived during the needs assessment may not always be in synchronization with the chosen unit of performance. For example, the total number of sales representatives may be ninety, but the unit of performance may be recorded by sales region, not by the number of individuals in the specified region. If this is the case and there are five sales regions, five is the number of participating *groups*. In contrast, if the unit of performance is dollars of sales per individual salesperson, the number of participants would be ninety. The number of participants is recorded on line *g* of the worksheet.

Work Performance During the HRD Program

The calculations for forecasting the performance value of an HRD program, items *h* through *m*, are fairly straightforward and mechanical. With the exception of item *h*, all the calculations use the data you have already entered in the upper portion of the performance value worksheet. Item *h* addresses the issue of work performance *during* the HRD program:

(h) *Usable units the worker/group/system produce during the HRD program?*

If no, enter "0". If yes, enter known performance rate or calculate average performance rate $[(b + c)/2]$.

Imagine that four new executives are hired by a *Fortune* 500 firm. The executives are sent with twenty others to a prestigious university for an intensive three-month development program that has been especially designed for the firm. The four new executives do not engage in any work of value to the firm during this period.

A rival firm across town also hires four new executives. The second firm provides just one week of orientation, analyzes each new executive's expertise, negotiates specific work goals with them in their areas of expertise, and provides in-house executive development programs using top executives and local professors who conduct theory-to-practice sessions during the first month that the new executives are employed. The new executives clearly add value to the firm during their development programs. Their performance levels during the HRD program can be plotted as rising stair steps.

I witnessed a simple model of performance during development years ago in an organization that provided apprenticeship training. There I saw trainees learning hand tool skills and directing their efforts toward producing small parts, all of which in the future would be made by machine in the factory. The purpose of the program was to provide an incentive for learning and to challenge the trainees to match the standards of machine-made products. As limited as the quantity of their production was, the parts they produced during training were salable. They had value.

The main question here is whether valued work performance units will be accomplished during the development program. If the answer is yes, the rate and timing of that performance during the HRD intervention must be determined. Short-term programs that pull people off the job and away from the work site usually yield zero units of performance during the HRD program.

There are two approaches to accounting for situations that combine development and performance:

- Enter the known performance rate.
- Calculate the average performance rate.

The first approach, entering the known performance rate, acknowledges the fact that HRD programs may conclude with work performances at less-than-goal levels. This is often true where further on-the-job practice will lead to performance at the expected rate. Some HRD options will yield a known number of units of performance at the end of the development period. In this case, enter the known performance numbers on line h of Figure 4.1. To help you visualize various patterns of work performance in structured and unstructured HRD programs, I have shown several plausible options in graphic form (Figure 4.4).

The second approach allows the forecaster to enter the average performance rate for the HRD options. Studies have shown that where employees are developed on the job in an unstructured manner, they produce at a rate of 50 percent or less during the development period (Cullen, Sisson, Sawzin, and Swanson, 1976). Again, this is a conservative estimate. Most practitioners believe that the actual rate is lower than this. Even so, if employees work at the 50 percent level for even short periods of time, this becomes a very expensive method of developing human resources.

For example, let's say a salesperson is expected to manage twelve accounts. Company records show that it has taken, on average, sixteen months for new salespeople to get to this level of performance when they are left to an unstructured HRD program of on-the-job self-development. Organizational performance records may be specific enough for you to calculate the average of actual performance rates for sixteen months. If not, using the average performance rate method $[(b + c)/2]$ yields an average performance of six accounts for new salespeople over the sixteen-month period $[(12 + 0)/2 = 6)]$.

In summary, the performance rate during the development period is entered on line h of the worksheet. If no performance is expected, the number entered should be zero. If there is performance and the rate is known, that number should be entered. If there is performance and the rate is not known, it should be estimated at the 50 percent performance level over the development period.

Total Performance During the HRD Program

Item i of the performance value worksheet (Figure 4.1) asks that all performance during the HRD program for each worker, group, or system be accounted for.

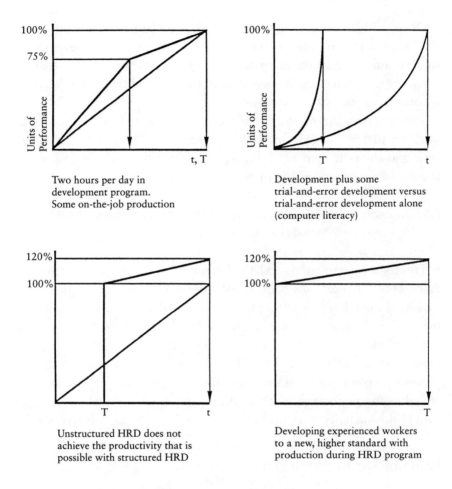

FIGURE 4.4   Variations on Performance Over Time During HRD Programs

(i) What are the total units per worker/group/system produced during the development time (h x e)?

Question i is answered for each HRD option being considered. With the formula (h x e), the rate of performance during the development time is multiplied by the amount of time (in development) required to reach the expected performance level. The product of this multiplication is entered on line i of the worksheet.

The next question on the worksheet, item *j*, differs from the previous question in a very important manner. The focus is on a fixed period of time and the estimated *total* performance over that period of time for the individual or group. The question reads:

(j) How many units will be produced per worker/group/system during the assessment period (i + [(f – e) x b])?

This fixed assessment period, the longest of all the development times among the HRD options being considered, provides the basis for comparing all the HRD program options. The formula for *j* determines how many units of time remain after the development period to the end of the assessment period *(f – e)* and then multiplies this number times the expected full performance level (b). The total time of working at full performance *after* completion of the HRD program *[(f – e) x b]* is then added to the performance achieved *during* the HRD program *(i)*. The sum of this total performance is units during the full *assessment* period.

Value of Performance During Assessment Period

Item *k* of the worksheet (Figure 4.1) converts the total expected performance units to be accomplished (by individual workers, groups, or the system) into dollars:

(k) What is the value of the worker/group/system performance during the assessment period (j x d)?

The answer is obtained simply by multiplying the number of units, line *j*, times the dollar value of a single unit, line *d*. The result is the total dollar value of the worker or group's performance during the assessment period.

Performance Value Gain per Worker/Group/System

The gain in performance is the remaining calculation. The idea is to make sure not to take credit for any performance achieved before the HRD program is put into place. Item *l* of the worksheet pursues the performance value gain per worker, group, or system.

(l) What is the performance value gain per worker/group/system?
$$[k - (c \times d \times f)]$$

The formula for *l* is dominated by c, the performance at the beginning of the HRD program. When it is zero, the formula plays itself out as "*k* – *zero*," which equals *k*. If the beginning performance is greater than zero, the formula acknowledges this beginning performance level and does not allow the HRD program to accept unearned credit for it.

Total Performance Value Gain

At last I come to the item in which the HRD manager is most keenly interested. Item m tells us to compute the performance value gain for all workers/groups/systems as a result of the HRD program:

(m) What is the total performance value gain for all
workers/groups/systems (l x g)?

Once again, the calculation is a simple one. The performance value per worker/group/system *(l)* is multiplied by the number of workers/groups/systems *(g)*.

The source of many of the items on the performance value worksheet can be illustrated graphically. The performance time graph (Figure 4.3) illustrates for comparison two HRD program options. The first is the longer, unstructured HRD option. The second is the shorter, structured HRD option. Both options show production during the development time. This is a common pattern of development and production. Figure 4.4 illustrates a variety of productivity patterns during the development period. All the information needed to fill out the performance value worksheet is contained in the following description.

Conclusion

The following practical tips are to help you as you begin to assess the financial benefits of an HRD program:

- Work with a partner. Having someone to "talk through" assessments will provide support and reassurance.
- Use a pencil with a big eraser and have extra performance value worksheets at hand.
- Have a calculator handy.
- Record all information in the order in which you receive it. Don't let the order of the items on the worksheet get in your way.
- Beginning assessors find it easier to work all the way through one HRD option forecast at a time.
- It is important to work with knowledgeable experts to obtain and verify your numbers. Make phone calls or get up from your desk and seek out individuals who can supply the information you need.
- When in doubt, use the finest scale that is readily available. For example, use hours instead of days and calculate dollars in tens rather than in hundreds. Your numbers can be rounded off later.

Determining performance value is the most complex part of the forecasting process. Additional help follows in the form of five cases presented in the next chapter. Several components are provided for each case, including the situation, the performance value analysis, and a critique. These five cases will also appear after the costs and benefits chapters that follow.

Calculating the Cost

5

M ost discussions about the economics of human resource development (HRD) begin with costs. This is unfortunate. To decision
makers who understand economics and return on investment, costs can
be interpreted only in terms of the financial benefits of HRD. The ultimate purpose of this book is to refocus HRD financial discussions from
costs to *benefits*. Even so, costs must be calculated to answer bigger financial benefit questions.

"How much will it cost?" "What will we have to spend on that program?" In many organizations, managers view the HRD department as
nothing more than a financial burden. To them, HRD is a drain on earnings, not an investment in performance improvement of future capability of the organization. Through the calculation of *performance value,*
however, HRD interventions can be seen as enhancing the performance
of individuals, groups, and the organization. In this chapter, a worksheet
to aid in calculating HRD costs is presented. The purpose of the worksheet is to gather all the cost information needed to calculate the cost
portion of the basic financial assessment model.

Credibility Is Essential

Current practices include a variety of methods for assigning the costs of
HRD interventions. In some organizations the HRD department is designated a cost center; in others it is designated a profit center. Sometimes
HRD is buried in the personnel department, and some organizations do
not assign any costs at all to HRD programs at the corporate level.

HRD as a Cost Center.   A cost center is a point in the accounting records at which costs associated with a department or intervention are collected. All expenditures that are connected with a cost center are collected, recorded by category, and presented for review. When HRD is designated as a cost center, the HRD manager tends to concentrate on keeping the costs of essential HRD programs as low as possible. A major concern is how to implement programs in less expensive ways. Thus, when HRD is a cost center, efficiency can become more important than effectiveness. For example, orientation programs tend to shrink until they are two hours long, and new employees are left to learn the values and mores of the organization by other means. Usually, line management picks up at least some of the costs of HRD programs. Extended meetings, telephone time, downtime on production machinery, and salaries paid while supervisors participate in organization development interventions are allocated under various line items in operations. When line managers are not convinced of the value of HRD, they may claim an inability to find the funds to pay for proposed HRD programs unless "corporate will pay for it." When this happens, HRD dollars shrink still more.

HRD as a Profit Center.   Some HRD departments have been assigned profit responsibilities. The HRD staff primarily works to develop programs that address the needs of the parent organization. In addition to this activity, staff members are expected to add to the profitability of the company by marketing the same programs to other organizations. The Acme HRD department, for example, becomes Acme HRD Systems with its own product development, marketing, and sales functions—and corporate expectations for profitable operations.

HRD as a Support Service to Operations.   More often, especially in smaller organizations, HRD programs compete with recruiting, benefits management, and records management for resources. The costs of HRD interventions are charged back to the department that requested them or they are buried in a variety of personnel accounts.

In all these circumstances, the "true" costs of specific HRD efforts can be difficult to determine even though accounted-for costs can be tracked. But this is history. For assessment purposes, thorough cost analyses are needed. No matter how the costs of past HRD programs have been recorded, HRD professionals need to use their analytical skills in gathering cost data for use in forecasting the costs of a proposed HRD program. Once this is understood, HRD managers have little trouble deciding how to forecast and where to assign intervention costs.

Thinking About Costs

Few would deny that HRD interventions are costly. The most visible costs are incurred during the implementation phase of an HRD program. Implementation expenses such as travel, meals, meeting rooms, and facilitators add up quickly. These expenses grow even larger as more and more people become involved in the effort. But implementation costs represent only part of the total costs of HRD interventions. Every phase of every intervention (analysis through assessment) brings its costs. In Chapter 4 you were introduced to a worksheet to use in calculating the performance value for a proposed program (see Figure 4.1). In this chapter a worksheet to use in calculating program costs is presented. The cost worksheet (Figure 5.1) can be customized to fit any HRD intervention or system. In the basic financial assessment model, total program costs are subtracted from the performance value to yield the expected economic benefit to the organization. How to handle these costs when presenting a report for an HRD program to management depends on the expectations of management. Needless to say, the confidence that comes from knowing the benefits expected to result from an HRD effort permits a certain integrity in analyzing and assessing the direct and indirect costs to be incurred by that activity.

Analyzing Costs

In comparison to the challenge of calculating the performance value of an HRD program, the task of assessing program costs seems relatively straightforward. But as is usually the case in such matters, nothing is as simple as it first appears. For example, how would you answer the following questions?

1. Should overhead, or burden, be included in HRD costs?

2. What are all the real costs of an HRD intervention?

3. Are all the costs included in your proposals and reports?

The answer to the first two questions is: *It all depends.* If your company customarily charges a certain cost item to HRD or another department, you will propose charging the costs the same way. For instance, all copy expenses may be charged to administration, regardless of which department incurred them. This distinction is explained later in the chapter. The answer to the third question is: *You ought to have a good estimate of the costs,* but the costs that you include in your proposals and reports to management depend on the custom of your company and on your situation. When you calculate costs, observe two principles:

- Don't leave out any major cost items.
- Don't include unnecessary or exaggerated cost items.

Violating the first principle can ruin the integrity of your calculations and destroy your credibility in an instant. One astute challenge from management about a missing cost item can raise suspicions that your calculations may not be a trustworthy foundation on which to base an important decision. Violating the second principle can lead to overestimating costs and can mean the difference between acceptance and rejection, celebration or disappointment.

Systemic analysis is the key to finding and calculating the essential cost items to be included in an HRD assessment. Before discussing the costs that will be incurred by HRD, here is a review of the language of costs.

What Is a Cost?

Of the several definitions of *cost* in *Webster's Third New International Dictionary,* two are of particular interest:

- "An item of outlay incurred in the operation of a business enterprise (as for the purchase of raw materials, labor, services, supplies) including depreciation and amortization of capital assets."

- "Whatever must be given, sacrificed, suffered, or forgone to secure a benefit or accomplish a result."

Sacrifice may be too strong a word, but the second definition describes the subjective feelings that decision makers often experience when they think about supporting and paying for HRD programs. A major premise of this book is that HRD professionals can begin to communicate with decision makers more clearly about the expected financial benefits and actual benefits of HRD. You can maximize the possibility that decision makers in your company will objectively review the costs and benefits of an HRD intervention option.

But the first definition of a cost—"an item of outlay that is *incurred in the operation of [HRD programs]*"—seems to fit our purposes better. From this definition arises the necessity for constructing a cost picture of each proposed HRD option. But when was the last time you talked about or even thought about amortizing a capital asset, that is, spreading its costs over time? Maybe never. Although *amortization* may not be part of your daily vocabulary, you should remain open to the possible necessity of calculating such items as direct and indirect costs, fixed and variable costs, and amortization. The goal is to present *accurate* and *appropriate* HRD proposals to decision makers. Fortunately, you don't have to do all the figuring yourself. Help is usually either a visit or a phone call away. An example will clarify the difference between simple and elaborate cost analysis.

In response to an identified performance goal, two internal HRD consultants proposed team-building programs for twenty-five managers of the Mentax Company. The first consultant was the picture of thoroughness: "I figure we'll need four meeting rooms in the Lake Building. Now let's see . . . the building is six years old and is expected to remain usable for twenty-four more years. It cost $1.3 million. Taxes are $7,000 per year; maintenance is $4,300 per year. And landscaping, which is expected to last ten years, cost $5,500. The four rooms come to about one-sixteenth of the building. So, dividing $1.3 million by thirty and adding $11,850 for taxes, maintenance, and landscaping will give the annual cost. Now I divide the thirty hours we expect to use the rooms by 2,000 hours and I get . . . "

The second consultant used more expedient methods: "I figure we'll need four meeting rooms in the Lake Building. I called the person who schedules the meeting rooms. He said we could figure on being charged $300 a day for the use of all four rooms or $200 for every morning that we have scheduled. So, ten morning meetings comes to $2,000 for facilities."

Whenever possible, use the second approach to calculate HRD costs. Even though it is simple, it is *accurate* and *appropriate*. As a busy HRD professional you have many important tasks to do. Making elaborate calculations about the use of facilities is the job of the facilities manager, who probably has the figures already prepared. Furthermore, figures supplied by the facilities manager or the comptroller will likely carry more credibility than the painstakingly calculated figures of the HRD manager.

Using Financial Terminology

When talking with decision makers, it is a good idea to use either standard financial terminology or the same terminology that they use. Your effectiveness in communicating your HRD proposals increases greatly when you learn to use cost terminology that will be understood by the decision makers in your company.

What Is an HRD Cost?   An HRD cost is any expenditure that the organization chooses to attribute to an HRD program. If the organization does not normally associate a particular cost—such as the cost of facilities, office supplies, or telephones—with an HRD program, even though that cost might legitimately be charged to HRD, it *does not* have to be included in a forecast of costs of the program. What is considered an HRD cost in one organization may not necessarily be considered an HRD cost in another. Some costs are fixed no matter how many programs the HRD department runs. Some costs vary. Some costs can be directly attributed to specific HRD programs. Some cannot. I describe these and other cost terms and categories next.

Fixed Costs.   These are costs that are incurred no matter how many programs the HRD department produces. HRD staff salaries, office rent, utilities, and insurance are fixed costs. Two video decks, one in the conference room and one that travels from division to division with a set of videotapes on using performance appraisal techniques, may represent either a fixed cost of the HRD department or a variable cost directly attributable to a program. Employing a secretary at a salary of $20,000 plus 25 percent fringe benefits incurs a fixed cost of $25,000 to the HRD department. If the HRD department erects a facility in which to conduct its programs, its fixed costs could rise dramatically. A thorough analysis of HRD costs will identify a baseline set of fixed costs that will not vary directly with the number of programs or the number of participants.

Variable Costs. These costs generally increase or decrease with the number of programs run or participants involved. Each additional program entails costs, such as travel to conduct a performance diagnosis. The fewer the number of programs, the lower these costs will be. Variable costs increase as participation in HRD programs increases. Each additional participant incurs a package of costs that may include, for example, the costs of handouts, manuals, coffee, lunches, travel, and lodging. The greater the number of participants, the greater the variable costs.

Direct Costs. These are expenditures that are directly attributable to a specific program. Such costs would not exist if the program did not exist. For example, handout materials, printed brochures, and the labor of the outside vendor who produces them are direct costs to the program with which they are associated. Such costs are usually charged to the individual HRD program that incurs them.

Indirect Costs. These costs are associated with keeping the HRD department operating. They may be fixed costs or they may rise and fall with the level of activity in the department. Indirect costs are expenditures that are not directly attributable to a specific program. Hiring a second secretary, repainting a classroom, and renting a copy machine are indirect costs that are not fixed costs. They are also not chargeable to a specific program. Indirect costs tend to be invisible to the user of HRD. The HRD manager's salary, office supplies for the HRD department, and the monthly telephone bills are indirect costs. Slide and overhead projectors that are used or made available for *all* programs are indirect costs. Some program costs, such as outlays for paper and pencils, may be considered indirect because the amount of these materials used for any one program is too small to justify the expense of allocating them to individual programs. Sometimes HRD is charged with proportional costs for expensive items such as audiovisual equipment or furnishings. These indirect costs are too large to be paid for by individual programs. Such costs are written off over a period of ten or more years through regular charges to the department. They appear as a line item on yearly or monthly budgets.

Indirect costs of HRD may be charged to the corporate administration or personnel budgets or they may be charged proportionately to all the HRD programs for the year. For instance, in some organizations travel is put into a general travel account. In other organizations, travel is itemized according to who is traveling to what destination for what reason. In these organizations, travel for HRD and travel for sales would be recorded differently.

Charge-Backs and Overhead. The profit-making functions in organizations must eventually pay for HRD programs. In other words, HRD programs are a cost that burdens manufacturing or other line activities. Operations pay for HRD through charge-backs and through overhead. When a program is designed for and delivered to operations, the receiving department may agree to pick up the bill for travel, meals, and lodging for all participants. In addition, it may agree to be charged for facilitator fees, participant materials, and other program-specific costs. These costs are "charged back" to the receiving department. The receiving department may or may not be expected to pay for the costs of the needs assessment, the organization and job analysis, or the use of meeting rooms. Such expenditures could be charged to profit-generating operations through overhead.

Marginal Costs and Step Costs. These terms are not commonly used, but they are important to keep in mind when delivering a proposal to management. A marginal cost is the change in outlay that occurs when another participant is added to the program roster. Sometimes, however, no marginal cost occurs when more participants are added. For example, if a management consultant will speak to seventy executives for $5,000, the marginal cost for the seventy-first and seventy-second executives in attendance will probably be zero. The speaker will charge no more for two extra people. Thus, the financial assessor can often assume some flexibility in costs when adding a few more participants to a particular HRD activity.

Step costs rise incrementally. The cost of a team-building program will remain constant when ten to twenty people will be involved. But if we add a twenty-first person, it may be necessary to find a larger room and run another printing of handouts. The larger room and the additional run of handouts will take care of thirty people. But if we add a thirty-first person, we may again have to make other arrangements. And so on through stair-step changes in costs. As you develop your calculations, keep in mind the flexibilities and rigidities of cost patterns.

The listing of cost terms is by no means complete, but it will suffice to alert you to the need to understand and use managerial language when forecasting the costs of proposed programs. For the appropriate cost terminology in your particular organization, you might look to written material such as other successful proposals, departmental budgets, financial statements, and monthly productivity reports. In addition, you could interview other department heads that have successfully presented proposals to management. What cost terminology did they use? Please note that the essence of wisdom is to ask knowledgeable others to review your proposal before taking it to a meeting of decision makers.

There are no right or wrong ways to talk about costs. You are trying to make sure that your cost items are consistent with the customary cost categories in your company. You will want to include the cost items that the decision makers in your company are sure to be concerned about. You must decide whether to include a portion of HRD annual fixed (indirect) costs in your proposal or whether to exclude such costs because they would be considered irrelevant to the proposed program. For example, if administration generally lends its meeting rooms for your programs, meeting room costs will not appear on your forecasted cost analysis worksheet.

Cost Worksheet

HRD can be viewed as a process as well as a program. Direct costs arise during every phase of the systematic phases of the process that HRD professionals employ. The general process of HRD typically consists of five phases with variations:

Human Resource Development	Personnel Training and Development	Organization Development
1. Analyze	1. Analyze	1. Analyze/Contract
2. Propose	2. Design	2. Diagnose
3. Create	3. Develop	3. Plan
4. Implement	4. Implement	4. Implement
5. Assess	5. Evaluate	5. Evaluate/ Institutionalize

These are fairly standard terms for each of the phases. You may describe your systematic HRD practices with other process terms. Those are the terms and categories you should use and stick to. For accurate calculations, the expenses that will be associated with each HRD phase must be estimated and totaled. Most HRD interventions involve all phases. Purchased programs are the exception to this rule because the phases are lumped into the total purchase price of the package or into the fee charged by the external consultant. Even so, customizing a standard HRD program to meet the specific needs of your company will incur costs. Such costs will be assigned to the development phase. The basic cost worksheet is a useful guide for analyzing when and where most direct costs will be incurred by a proposed HRD intervention. There are three versions for the three HRD process variations (Figures 5.1, 5.2, and 5.3).

Discussion of the Cost Worksheet, Personnel Training, and Development Illustration

High-quality human resource development comes about in the process of meeting critical organizational needs. For this reason, identifying specific performance requirements is one goal of the first phase of the personnel training and development (T&D) process. For example, the T&D manager travels to a subsidiary to interview several people about a problem they have identified. Once there, the manager finds that the data input people are making numerous mistakes in categorizing certain types of information. The analyst discovers that there are two reasons for these er-

Program/Intervention _____ Analyst _____ Date _____

	Option name	1 _____	2 _____
Analyze			
Step 1	_____	_____	_____
Step 2	_____	_____	_____
Step 3	_____	_____	_____
Step 4	_____	_____	_____
Propose			
Step 1	_____	_____	_____
Step 2	_____	_____	_____
Step 3	_____	_____	_____
Step 4	_____	_____	_____
Create			
Step 1	_____	_____	_____
Step 2	_____	_____	_____
Step 3	_____	_____	_____
Step 4	_____	_____	_____
Implement			
Step 1	_____	_____	_____
Step 2	_____	_____	_____
Step 3	_____	_____	_____
Step 4	_____	_____	_____
Assess			
Step 1	_____	_____	_____
Step 2	_____	_____	_____
Step 3	_____	_____	_____
Step 4	_____	_____	_____
<u>Total HRD costs</u>		$ _____	$ _____
		(Option 1)	(Option 2)

FIGURE 5.1   Cost Worksheet: Human Resource Development

Program/Intervention _____ Analyst _____ Date _____

Option name	1 _____	2 _____
Analyze:		
Diagnose performance	_____	_____
Document expertise	_____	_____
Other _____	_____	_____
Other _____	_____	_____
Design:		
Design program	_____	_____
Design lessons	_____	_____
Other _____	_____	_____
Other _____	_____	_____
Develop:		
Develop materials	_____	_____
Pilot test program	_____	_____
Other _____	_____	_____
Other _____	_____	_____
Implement:		
Manage program	_____	_____
Deliver training	_____	_____
Other _____	_____	_____
Other _____	_____	_____
Evaluate:		
Assess results	_____	_____
Report results	_____	_____
Other _____	_____	_____
Other _____	_____	_____
<u>Total T&D costs</u>	$ _____	$ _____
	(Option 1)	(Option 2)

FIGURE 5.2   Cost Worksheet: Personnel Training and Development

Program/Intervention _____ Analyst _____ Date _____

Option name	1 _____	2 _____
1. *Analyze & Contract*		
Analyze	_____	_____
Contract	_____	_____
Other _____	_____	_____
Other _____	_____	_____
2. *Diagnose & Feedback*		
Diagnose	_____	_____
Feedback	_____	_____
Other _____	_____	_____
Other _____	_____	_____
3. *Plan Design & Develop*		
Plan design	_____	_____
Develop	_____	_____
Other _____	_____	_____
Other _____	_____	_____
4. *Implement*		
Manage	_____	_____
Deliver	_____	_____
Other _____	_____	_____
Other _____	_____	_____
5. *Evaluate & Institutionalize*		
Evaluate results	_____	_____
Institutionalize	_____	_____
Other _____	_____	_____
Other _____	_____	_____
Total OD costs	$	$
	(Option 1)	(Option 2)

FIGURE 5.3   Cost Worksheet: Organization Development

rors. First, the clerks lack an understanding of how the data will be used. Second, the system that they are working with is unusually complex. The analyst interviews several supervisors of the data input clerks. They verify the need for redesigning (simplifying) at least a part of the work system and for special training for the part of the job that cannot be redesigned. Performance diagnosis activities are part of the analysis phase. What follows is an overview of cost calculations using the typical personnel training and development phase categories of analyze, design, develop, implement, and evaluate.

Analysis Phase.   Managers often recognize and voice the need for a training program to deal with a particular problem in the organization—perhaps noticeable friction among top managers or a lawsuit over sexual harassment may highlight the need for an HRD training program. Typically, you or your consultant will personally investigate the problem before beginning to design a solution.

During this analysis phase, staff costs will be incurred whenever you use observations, interviews, or surveys or whenever you gather and review organizational records for purposes of collecting and recording baseline data. A thorough performance diagnosis can require quite a commitment of staff time. In a large organization, interviewing the people who are concerned with the problem or opportunity could take several days and involve travel. Expenses for materials during the analysis phase will be added if you intend to conduct a formal survey. Postage and sundry expenditures will be anticipated. Sometimes copies of organizational records will be gathered. On occasion, you will hire an external consultant to conduct a more sophisticated or more objective performance diagnosis than the capabilities of the internal staff will allow. The consultant's fee is entered as a cost of the analysis phase, as are his or her travel and lodging expenses and any support services that are anticipated. The major result of this analysis phase is a proposal for both HRD and management actions to address a specific performance need. Some secretarial help may be needed to prepare the proposal for presentation to management.

Sometimes, when the HRD need is for technical skills training—for example, when new machinery or new work systems are anticipated—analysis of work behavior will be required. Job descriptions and task analyses must be recorded and task analyses must be carried out. Be aware that documenting work expertise can be a time-consuming task.

Perhaps an analysis of a subject area is indicated. For example, a review of the literature on performance appraisal may be planned. New, well-researched appraisal methods will be used to evaluate the appraisal system currently in use in your company. Examining the performance appraisal process in the work setting and conducting a literature search take a lot of time. But careful analytical work yields useful material for inclusion in a performance management program. Miscellaneous cost items in the analysis phase will include secretarial service for typing and research assistance for gathering library materials.

Design Phase.   The primary task of the design phase is planning the details of the T&D program. Because this work primarily requires the expertise of the HRD professional, few costs other than the cost of the designer's time will be involved. Nevertheless, this cost can be significant. The designer will take into account such variables as the number and characteristics of program participants, the objectives to be achieved, and the process to achieve them. Designing a program, outlining the progression of activities, and working through the details of what people must do to achieve the desired results of the training program can involve a lot of careful, detailed thinking. Perhaps an off-the-shelf program will accomplish the same goals. But research to find just the right package or one that can be tailored to the company and to the specific performance goal also takes time.

Development Phase.   In this phase, the materials that will be used during the T&D program are created, purchased, or located. Such materials include job aids, films, value clarification instruments, and participant packets. If expensive media are to be used for the training program, costs could rise dramatically. Creating a video, a slide and tape show, or a job reference manual calls for the use of expensive artistic and writing skills. Creating an interactive video or computer-based instruction program could require up to 200 hours of development time for every hour of running time. When your department does not have the talent needed to develop the proposed media, you will have to hire artists, instructional designers, and scriptwriters, and you may also have to rent studios. Developing pretests and post-tests, as well as pilot testing and revising HRD programs, involves additional costs that you must anticipate for this phase.

Implementation Phase. Here we find ourselves in the more visible portion of the iceberg of T&D costs. Most decision makers recognize the necessity of paying for facilitators and instructors, travel to and from a training session, meals and lodging, paper and pencils for assessing management styles, and a television monitor for picking up remote programs via satellite. These costs are significant, but the largest HRD costs that will be incurred during the implementation phase are the salaries of participants. Twenty managers attending a strategic planning workshop for a day can ring up quite a bill for their time. But unlike hourly employees who attend HRD programs, managers may be expected to make up the work they miss. No work left undone means no charge for salaries to the HRD program. As a calculator of costs, you must anticipate making such cost decisions.

Sending executives to MBA programs and machine operators to vestibule training can also lead to costs in the form of tuition, materials, and fees. Career development programs involve costs for tests and counseling. All such costs are forecasted under the implementation phase. Given the extensive participant costs incurred during the implementation phase, staffing costs incurred during this phase can seem quite modest. Thus, the direct costs of staff to deliver a training program may appear small. In contrast, the direct cost of materials used may be quite high, especially if the cost of mistakes made on the way to learning important work skills is counted. The costs of books, manuals, handouts, and other consumable items must be estimated and the cost of distributing information about the T&D program and meals for participants.

Evaluation Phase. If a program involves a large investment or management wants to look at the T&D record later, the advantages of assessing training programs becomes quite clear. In the press of trying to determine costs for other program phases, however, practitioners sometimes neglect to add the costs that will be incurred during the evaluation phase. Following up on the results of training deserves at least as much attention as the other program phases. Ideally, three successive domains of assessment will be pursued to determine the results of an HRD intervention, and each involves costs (see Swanson and Holton, 1999).

First, what are the participants' and stakeholders' perceptions of the results of the T&D program? Designing, administering, collecting, and compiling participant perception ratings take staff time. The perception ratings of the supervisors or executives who requested and paid for the HRD effort must also be gathered, compiled, and analyzed.

Second, what new knowledge and behaviors or what new expertise has been gained as a result of the program? Creating, administering, and scoring measures of knowledge and expertise take staff time. Materials costs could also be incurred as new abilities to understand concepts, manipulate machines, and complete paperwork are demonstrated.

Third, what changes in individual, group, or organization performance can be expected to occur as the result of the HRD program? Measures of performance results will be gathered and compared with the baseline data to be collected during the performance diagnosis phase. Staff time will be needed either to make or to follow up on these measurements.

Converting performance measures and whatever it takes to achieve them into dollars and cents is the financial benefit level of performance results assessment. Assessing financial benefits is *forecasted* in the initial HRD phase. Actual financial benefit assessment is done throughout the phases. These *actual* figures can be compared with the *forecasted* figures. Comparing actual performance values and actual costs and benefits with forecasted performance values, costs, and benefits will aid you in improving your forecasting skills. In addition, *approximated* financial cost calculations can be conducted at the final assessment or evaluation phase without the availability of *forecasted* or *actual* assessments.

Total Direct and Indirect Costs.   There can be little doubt that HRD programs can be costly. The total of direct costs attributable to even a modest in-house program will often be larger than a first, quick estimate indicates. Look at the cost lists in Figures 5.1, 5.2, and 5.3 as a memory jogger whenever you complete the cost worksheet for an HRD program.

Consistency Is Needed

The performance value worksheet (Figure 4.1) and the costs worksheet are used together. One complements the other. The HRD professional needs both worksheets to form a true picture of each option under consideration. Experience shows that it is better to complete the performance value worksheet for an option before attempting to calculate the costs for that option. One caution about filling in the cost worksheet is in order: it must be compiled with data that are consistent with those of the performance value worksheet. When filling out one of the two worksheets on the basis of a total program, the other should be filled out on the same basis. Both worksheets can also be filled out per organization system, group, or individual worker. Just be sure to focus on the group or system that will be involved in the HRD activity.

One more area of consistency is important. When determining costs, you may find that the managers in your company do not agree on which items to include on the cost sheet and what dollar costs should be assigned to them. It is important to use a consistent framework for bounding each option under consideration. Without close attention to this detail, you could end up comparing the proverbial apples and oranges instead of two comparable HRD options. It is worth developing a customized cost analysis worksheet that matches your HRD process and your organization's cost accounting practices.

Depending on the custom in your company, you may want to estimate the total amount of the indirect costs (see previous discussion on cost terminology) of the HRD department and add a portion of these to the program cost at the bottom of the worksheet.

Conclusion

In this chapter, cost terminology as it is used in many organizations has been defined. Most HRD costs are easy to uncover but some can be found only after careful digging. Asking the right people for pertinent cost figures and knowing what HRD costs the decision makers expect to see on your assessments are important to your success in the role of assessor. Completing *the* cost worksheet is generally an easier task than completing the performance value worksheet, but don't be casual about this task. In Chapters 7, 8, and 9 there are several case examples with completed cost worksheets.

Calculating the Benefit

The basic financial assessment model includes methods for determining financial values for the following components: the *performance value* resulting from the HRD program, the *cost* of the HRD program, and the *benefit* resulting from the HRD program. Calculating the benefit is the ultimate act of simplicity—subtract the cost from the performance value to derive the financial benefit.

Two Views of Benefits

Gene Williams is the HRD director for a service organization in a fast-moving and highly competitive market. Everybody likes Gene, and he knows it. He is very skilled at using his likable personality to achieve what he thinks is best for his company. Like that of many HRD professionals, much of Gene's success is related to his ability to listen, empathize, and meet the expectations of management. No question about it, Gene has been successful. One indicator of this success is his becoming director of HRD in less than five years. Some time ago, however, Gene realized that he was not included in the critical decisionmaking activities of his company. He felt stymied in his goal to contribute more to company decisions.

A few years back Gene had taken a major step toward this goal by beginning to learn about the economics of human development. After several discussions with a colleague from another firm, Gene decided that he could assume greater career risks on behalf of his company. He resolved to:

- Propose an HRD program that would respond directly to a *strategic business need,* not just to a *management want.*

- Include a *forecasted financial benefit* of this HRD program in his proposal to management and agree to assess the *actual financial benefit* of the program at its conclusion.

Both of these actions took some courage. Both were clearly outside Gene's generally recognized professional strengths, and both were departures from current HRD practice. To be honest, though, any real risk to Gene's career was mitigated somewhat by his private resolve to seek employment elsewhere unless some expansion of his role in his company was forthcoming.

Gene's company had lost a significant percentage of its market share to a new competitor. After the board of directors had studied the company's annual business plans and reported its observations of various operations throughout the company, it concluded that improved customer service could significantly improve sales volume. The directors agreed with Gene that a major HRD effort to alter the present corporate approach to customer service was required. Gene's investigation yielded the following forecast figures for the proposed customer service program:

Performance Value	$200,000
- Cost	$50,000
Benefit	$150,000

The forecasted benefit was significant. A 4-to-1 return on investment (ROI) for the HRD program could be realized in twelve months. With such figures in hand, Gene easily gained support for the proposed customer service HRD program. Because Gene used extremely conservative estimates for his calculations, it was no surprise to him that the *actual* return on investment at the conclusion of the program was a ROI of 6:1, or a $300,000 performance value for a $50,000 investment. Almost overnight, Gene moved into the inner circle of decisionmakers in his firm.

Gene has become convinced that two different views of the expected results of HRD can be blended into one powerful HRD package. He has not lost the traditional "people skills" of HRD. In fact, his ideas about human development are more widely shared among the people in his firm than ever before as a result of their being exposed to the content of the customer service program. Although his new economic perspective on the "human capital" of the firm might have been less than characteristic of his thinking a short time ago, he now talks about human resources as worthy of investment. He believes that the smart business invests in and takes care of its people. Gene talks with ease to management about these things in their own language—the language of dollars and cents—every time he proposes a program and reports results.

Opportunity

The opportunity to talk about the financial costs and benefits of HRD is available to every HRD professional. In Gene Williams's case, the pressure to change came from within himself. In other instances, the pressure to change may come from management or from peers. Generally, the pressure for financial results comes from the top as executives begin to ask their HRD staff what real value their department is contributing to the organization. Interestingly, and fortunately for HRD, the same executives hold relatively modest expectations for HRD's adding value to the company. Working in such circumstances of high pressure and low expectations leads the HRD staff to ask, "We know what HRD can do for our company, but will management believe any assessment benefit greater than other high-performing investments?"

Benefit Computation

The benefit computation is a simple subtraction activity recorded on the benefit worksheet (Figure 6.1).

Positive Benefits.   Benefit figures can be examined from several perspectives. The first is to note if the calculated benefit is a positive one. Does the performance value of the proposed HRD program exceed the total costs of the program? Breaking even is acceptable; anything more is gravy. An

Date _____

Program/Intervention _____ Analyst _____

Option	1 _____	2 _____
Performance Value	$ _____	$ _____
Minus Cost	_____	_____
Benefit	$ _____	$ _____

NOTE: Circle your choice of option.

FIGURE 6.1   Benefit Worksheet

assessed benefit of a 1 to 1 measurable return on an HRD investment can represent value to the organization—return on investment (ROI) of 1:1. If the forecast for performance value and cost is made conservatively, there is always the potential for a return greater than 1 to 1. In fact, many studies of systematic HRD interventions focused on performance requirements yielded 8:1 ROI in a year or less (see Swanson, 1998; Appendix B). Furthermore, many HRD programs also can be expected to yield such nonfinancial benefits to the organization as strengthening the culture and encouraging a better understanding of its traditions.

Relative Benefits.   When two or more HRD options are available to address a performance problem, the general financial assessment model offers an easy method for deciding between them. The following hypothetical numbers will illustrate this point:

If we were to look only at the hypothetical financial benefits, Option 2 would clearly be the best investment choice. The Option 2 benefit of $188,000 can be compared directly with the benefit of $90,000 for Option 1 and $75,000 for Option 3. In a cash-short organization, however, the relatively small advantage of Option 1, the unstructured HRD pro-

	Option 1 *Unstructured*	Option 2 *Structured*	Option 3 *Structured*
Performance Value	$90,000	$288,000	$225,000
- Cost	- 0	- 100,000	- 150,000
Benefit	$90,000	$188,000	$75,000

FIGURE 6.2   Hypothetical Financial Numbers

gram, over Option 3, a structured program, will appear quite attractive. Because unstructured HRD incurs no direct costs, it will not cut into already limited cash resources. Furthermore, unstructured HRD requires little or no change in organizational operations.

Return on Investment.   The third perspective is to review the return on investment. ROI is simply a ratio that expresses the relationship of every dollar of performance value to every dollar expended to achieve that value. The return on investment for each option is obtained by dividing the forecast performance value by the forecast cost. If not otherwise stated, we assume that return on investment is based on a one-year period. For example, a 2 to 1 ratio means that $2 is returned for every $1 invested in a program in a one-year period. Most forecasts will be based on the longest HRD option under scrutiny. The returns on investment for our three options are:

- Option 1: ROI 0 to 0   (0:0)
- Option 2: ROI 2.88 to 1   (2.88:1)
- Option 3: ROI 1.5 to 1   (1.5:1)

By calculating returns on investment, you can compare the return ratio from any investment to HRD investments as well as compare each alternative HRD intervention meant to achieve performance goals. In this way, investments in human resources can be compared with each other and with non-HRD investments such as new machinery, new work methods, or other performance improvement efforts.

Reduced Benefit As a Cost

Sara Chu is director of human resources for the Malaysia Broadcast Network (MBN), a fast-growing communication-technology Asian company. Sara has had to regularly confront the fact that MBN relies on very expensive expatriates to serve in the role of broadcast engineers. These key engineers create the designs and innovations that sustain and advance the business. The Malaysian workforce simply does not have engineers with the broadcast engineering expertise and MBN-specific expertise required. The options available to Sara and MBN are to continue to use expatriates or to develop the needed expertise in a group of Malaysian workers.

Although the training and development of Malaysian engineers seemed unrealistic in the past, Sara began running the numbers to reassess the situation. The cost of the ten expatriate engineers has been enormous. At $200,000 each for salary and housing, the total annual expenditure is $2 million. Qualified Malaysian engineers would require $75,000 annual salary and this would mean an annual compensation of $0.75 million dollars. The salarly gap between the two labor groups is $1.25 million. Sara began to explore optional strategies for developing Malaysian broadcast engineers to the level of expertise required by MBN. Several options emerged. Most involved overseas education and training as well as extensive apprenticing back at MBN. What Sara and MBN found was that even the most exotic and expensive development option still respresented a large savings for MBN. In that there was no room for slippage in performance, they were careful to plan for overdevelopment of the required expertise.

Throughout this book I have been talking about development, improvement, and performance gains. This perspective of HRD focuses on HRD as an investment in anticipation that performance values will exceed costs. The harsh reality is that there are rival visions of HRD:

- HRD as a major business process . . . *something an organization must do to succeed.*
- HRD as a value-added activity . . . *something that is potentially worth doing.*
- HRD as an optional activity . . . *something that is nice to do.*

- HRD as a waste of business resources . . . *something that has costs exceeding the benefits.* (Swanson, 1995, 207)

Implicit in this range of perspectives is the fact that a "benefit" in some situations can simply be cost savings, not a benefit in terms of performance gains. If the dominant financial perspective is only on costs, HRD potential is automatically capped. Even so, the profession is also challenged to meet the "first imperative to demonstrate that it can do the work better, faster, and cheaper than any other source" (Fitz-Enz, 2000, 191).

As noted earlier, talking about costs out of context of performance is crippling to the ideals of development and investment. This is an appropriate time in this book to talk about cost reduction as an avenue to benefit. It is appropriate at this point because every attempt has been made to talk about HRD as a driver of performance to be viewed through the benefit assessment model (performance value - cost = benefit).

HRD professionals who carry this benefit assessment model to the table when there are cost reduction goals will be fully equipped for the task. HRD professionals should regularly consider less costly alternatives to reach goals. To do this wisely, a clear understanding of performance and performance value is required. Imagine the following situation, where there is to be no change in the performance and performance value with a change in costs between two options:

	Existing Option	*New Option*
Performance Value	40,000	40,000
-Cost	- 10,000	- 8,000
Benefit	30,000	32,000
ROI	4:1	5:1

In the case above the cost reduction is a real saving because the performance value remained constant. It cannot be taken for granted that the performance value will remain constant. Another case could be a cost reduction of $5,000 from a $10,000 cost to a $5,000 cost. An attractive savings. Yet if the performance value dropped to $25,000, saving $5,000 would be foolish.

Thus, even if the financial agenda is to reduce costs, performance is the key. The goal, then, as a responsible steward of organizational funds, is to hold on to known performance values and work to reduce costs. Holding performance values constant allows the organization's standard cost accounting system to dominate as the database for comparing options.

If HRD is going to demonstrate that it can do the work better, faster, and cheaper than any other source, it will need to engage in financial benefit assessment. If HRD is going to become a strategic organizational partner in achieving present and future performance goals, it will need to engage in financial benefit assessment.

Conclusion

In this chapter, the calculation of benefits as used in many organizations has been defined. At first glance, completing the benefit analysis worksheet appears to be simple, and it is. Even so, variations in presenting the benefit data can be pursued. Variations include positive benefits, relative benefits, and returns on investment.

Forecasted Financial
Benefits—Case Examples

In this chapter two case situations of *forecasting* the financial benefits of human resource development (HRD) will be presented. Figure 1.2, Framework and Key Questions for Assessing HRD Financial Benefits, asks, What is the *forecasted* financial benefit resulting from an HRD intervention? This is the before-the-fact assessment based on forecasted financial data.

The purpose of including two cases from different contexts is twofold. First, it highlights the fact that the *forecasting* financial benefit method can be used in a wide variety of situations—from government and private sectors to manufacturing and service organizations. It can be used in any situation where HRD interventions contribute to the achievement of valued organizational goals. Second, the case examples are meant to increase your confidence that the *forecasting* method will work. For each case in this chapter there is a detailed description of the facts of the case, a critique of the facts, and completed performance value, cost, and benefit worksheets.

Manufacturing Case. Here, the *forecasting* method is used to help in choosing among several HRD options aimed at training production workers who turn out circuit boards (see Figures 7.1, 7.2, and 7.3).

Service Industry Case. Learning to use companies to conduct market analyses in the real estate business is the performance goal. For this case, we develop the performance values for three different HRD options (see Figures 7.4, 7.5, and 7.6).

Manufacturing Case: Forecasted Financial Benefits

Situation. Profit margins of a manufacturing company that makes specialized circuit boards had been declining. The top management team encouraged departments to participate in a companywide performance needs assessment. The major finding was that inspection rejected far too many of the circuit boards. All the production workers were trained through the unstructured on-the-job training method. It was furthermore discovered that this training method required forty days before a worker could produce three good boards every two days. On the average, the workers read at the fifth-grade level and they experienced difficulty with the English language.

In addition, ten new production workers were to be hired and would need circuit board training. The options facing management were to continue with the current unstructured training, to develop and deliver an in-house structured training program, or to contract with an experienced consulting training firm that promised to get the workers up to the performance goal in eight days. No circuit boards would be produced during either of the structured training options.

If the structured in-house option were selected, the training staff would team up with the chief electronic engineer to carry out the project. They estimated that in-house structured training would allow workers to reach the performance goal in ten days. Temporary clerical help would be hired to assist during the analysis, design, and development stages. The following additional information will help in analyzing this case:

1. Dollar value per board $600
2. Number of trainees   10
3. Performance goal   1.5 circuit boards per day
4. External consultant rate $2,220 per trainee

Critique. This is a straightforward financial forecasting case. The performance diagnosis clearly established a need that could be met by an

HRD circuit board training program. Each unit of work performance—a circuit board—is obviously attributable to an individual worker. It is also likely that production records are kept so that the number of days it takes new circuit board assembly workers to train themselves on the job is known. In this case it took forty days.

The production of usable units during Option 1 (unstructured training) was estimated by using the average rate formula. It is possible that available company records could have instead provided exact rates.

Since assembling circuit boards is labor intensive, the analyst expected that the company had a precise dollar value for each. It did. Just a few unproduced $600 circuit boards or a few boards going into the trash can add up to significant numbers. Both of the structured training programs promised to get the workers producing at the performance goal in relatively short periods of time—eight and ten days versus forty days. Therefore, over the entire evaluation period either of these options would yield about $10,000 of additional performance value per worker. Multiply this times ten workers, and the total net performance difference for the structured training options was about $100,000 more than for the unstructured option.

Forecasted Costs and Benefits. The manufacturing case focused on the problem of an unacceptably high rejection rate of expensive electronic circuit boards during their production. Structured technical training for production workers was determined to be an appropriate HRD response to this problem. Three HRD options were entertained in the forecast. They include keeping the existing unstructured on-the-job training, using an HRD consultant who specializes in electronics technical training, and developing a training program using in-house personnel.

From a strictly financial perspective, it is clear that the forecast benefit of $180,000 for the existing unstructured training option is unacceptable when compared to the forecast benefit of $265,800 for the consultant option and of $252,144 for the in-house development option (Figure 7.1).

From a benefits-only perspective, the in-house option offers only $13,656 less in benefit to the organization than the consultant option. This relatively insignificant difference leaves room to consider the other five HRD decision criteria—appropriateness, availability, quality, prior

Program/Intervention _Circuit Boards Training_ **Analyst** _____ **Date** _____

	Option name:	1 _Unstructured_	2 _In-House_	3 _Consultant_
Data required for calculations:				
(a) What unit of performance are you measuring?		_Boards (Bds.)_ unit name	_Boards (Bds.)_ unit name	_Boards (Bds.)_ unit name
(b) What is the performance goal per worker/group/system at the end of your HRD program?		_1.5_ _Bds._ / _Day_ no. units / time	_1.5_ _Bds._ / _Day_ no. units / time	_1.5_ _Bds._ / _Day_ no. units / time
(c) What is the performance per worker/group/system at the beginning of the HRD program?		_1.5_ _Bds._ / _Day_ no. units / time	_1.5_ _Bds._ / _Day_ no. units / time	_1.5_ _Bds._ / _Day_ no. units / time
(d) What dollar value is assigned to each performance unit?		$_600_ /unit	$_600_ /unit	$_600_ /unit
(e) What is the development time required to reach the expected performance level?		_40_ _Days_ no. time	_10_ _Days_ no. time	_8_ _Days_ no. time
(f) What is the assessment period? (Enter the longest time (e) of all options being considered.)		_40_ _Days_ no. time	_40_ _Days_ no. time	_40_ _Days_ no. time
(g) How many workers/groups/ systems will participate in your HRD program?		_10_ no.⟨workers⟩ groups/systems	_10_ no.⟨workers⟩ groups/systems	_10_ no.⟨workers⟩ groups/systems
Calculations to determine net performance value:				
(h) Usable units worker/group/system produce during the HRD program? If no, enter -0-. If yes, enter known performance rate or calculate average performance rate [$(b + c)/2$]		_.75_ _Bds._ no. units	_0_ _Bds._ no. units	_0_ _Bds._ no. units
(i) What are the total units per worker/group/system produced during the development time? ($h \times e$)		_30_ no. of units	_0_ no. of units	_0_ no. of units
(j) How many units will be produced per worker/work group/system during the assessment period? {[$(f - e) \times b$] + i}		_30_ no. of units $ _18,000_	_45_ no. of units $ _27,000_	_48_ no. of units $ _28,800_
(k) What is the value of the worker's/group's/system's performance during the assessment period? ($j \times d$)		$ _18,000_	$ _27,000_	$ _28,800_
(l) What is the performance value gain per worker/group/system? [$k - (c \times d \times f)$]		$ _180,000_	$ _270,000_	$ _288,000_
(m) What is the total performance value gain for all workers/groups/		(Option 1)	(Option 2)	(Option 3)

FIGURE 7.1   Performance Value Worksheet: Manufacturing Case

Program/Intervention *Manufacturing - Circuit Boards Training*   Analyst _____   Date _____

Option name	1 *Unstructured*	2 *In-House*	3 *Consultant*
Analyze:			
Performance Diagnosis		3,224	
Document Expertise		510	
Other _____			
Other _____			
Design:			
Design program		1,100	
Design training		2,400	
Other _____			
Other _____			
Develop:			
Develop materials		1,000	
Pilot test program		600	
Production and duplication		120	
Other _____			
Implement:			
Manage program		2,294	
Deliver program		5,760	22,200
Other _____			
Other _____			
Evaluate:			
Assess results		208	
Performance follow-up		600	
Other _____			
Other _____			
Total T&D costs	$ 0	$ 17,816	$ 22,200
	(Option 1)	(Option 2)	(Option 3)

FIGURE 7.2   Cost Worksheet: Manufacturing Case

effectiveness, and cost—for choosing the best option. In this case, the prior effectiveness and availability decision criteria emerged as issues. The managers were generally unimpressed with the consultant because he could provide little evidence of the prior effectiveness of his program. They were also concerned about his ability to deliver high-quality training in the midst of an already heavy client load. Given these concerns, the decisionmakers chose the in-house option.

An interesting side note to this cast is that this company had never made any direct expenditures for training of any employees at any level. Their psychological barriers included spending money for training and spending what they thought was a significant amount of money on people fairly low in the organization. It was the financial forecast that got them to accept the HRD proposal.

Date _____

Program/Intervention _Manufacturing - Circuit Boards Training_ Analyst_____

Option	1 _Unstructured_	2 _In-House_	3 _Consultant_
Performance Value	$ 180,000	$ 270,000	$ 288,000
Minus Cost	0	17,856	22,000
Benefit	$ 180,000	$ 252,144	$ 265,800

NOTE: Circle your choice of option.

FIGURE 7.3 Benefit Worksheet: Manufacturing Case

Service Industry Case: Forecasted Financial Benefits

Situation. The service organization you work for provides real estate market analyses for brokers. Business is expanding and you, the HRD director, have been asked to look closely at the people-performance issues related to executing market analyses and initiating a new hiring campaign.

Each analysis takes an hour to perform when it is executed by a competent analyst using a personal computer connected to a mainframe computer. There is a $70 fee for each analysis. Your company is about to hire twenty-five new analysts. Until now, new analysts were trained through an unstructured on-the-job method that required six weeks before the analyst was "up to speed." A "buddy" spent about twenty hours with a new analyst during this period.

The vendors who sold you the software program and trained the first ten analysts want to contract with you for additional development services. They could deliver training at their facility (105 miles away) over a three-day period. Their charge would include two consultants for each day of training and twenty days of development time.

For an in-house option you estimate seven full days (fifty-six hours) of training, with trainees being unable to produce usable market analyses during the development period. Experience has shown that it takes your department two hours of non-HRD expert time for each hour of structured training attributable to the project. Trainee and HRD staff time does not need to be covered. Costs available from company records include:

Salaries: Participants $24,000 to $28,000
   Administrative support $16,000 to $20,000
   HRD professionals $23,000 to $25,000
   Subject matter experts $26,000 to $32,000
   Miscellaneous support personnel $16,000 to $20,000
Fringe and overhead: 36 percent rate
Travel: 26 cents per mile; $40 per diem; $80 per night
Facilities: $75 per day for a minimum of twenty people off site;
   $50 per day for a maximum of thirty people on site
Maintenance: $50 per day on site
Equipment: PC purchase $4,000; PC rental $500 per week
Materials: Consumables $500; reusable $700
Outside services: fees $80 per hour; travel mileage plus hourly;
   direct costs estimated at 20 percent fee

Critique.   This company, which started small, formally oriented and trained its original employees in company values and work methods. In subsequent years, however, orientation training for new hires has relaxed into an unstructured "buddy" system. A new spurt of growth has management again thinking about providing structured training for its market analysts.

Although management is committed to structured training, the HRD staff felt it was important to analyze the existing unstructured conditions to retain perspective. The two structured options vary. One is three days long, the other is seven days long. One is on site, the other is off site. One yields usable products during training, the other does not. Even with the differences, this analysis is fairly straightforward. The unit of performance (market analysis) is clear and easily attributable to individual employees. The worth of the unit is known by the company.

Although the inefficiency of the existing unstructured development program is shocking, this is typical of fast-growing companies that do not take the time to analyze what is happening in the midst of their success.

Service Industry Case Costs and Benefits.   The service industry case demonstrates what happens in an organization that has let its HRD efforts slip over the years. Now the service company will have to hire twenty-five new employees to execute badly needed market analyses. Three options—unstructured, vendor-delivered, and in-house HRD— were considered in response to the immediate performance need of this organization.

The benefit forecast definitely seemed to favor the vendor option. The forecast clearly eliminated the low-cost, low-benefit unstructured option from consideration (Figure 7.3). The forecast $45,411 difference in benefits between the vendor option and the in-house option is significant. Decisionmakers would have to see some impressive gain from the five other decision criteria to reject this benefit. If there had been a critical problem of vendor availability, for example, the in-house option would have been the better option. Delaying the development of twenty-five hires is nearly unthinkable in a profit-making organization.

Option name:	1 _Unstructured_	2 _Vendor_	3 _In-House_
Data required for calculations:	_Market Analysis_	_Market Analysis_	_Market Analysis_
(a) What unit of performance are you measuring?	(M.A.) unit name	(M.A.) unit name	(M.A.) unit name
(b) What is the performance goal per worker/group/system at the end of your HRD program?	1 M.A. / Hr. no. units / time	1 M.A. / Hr. no. units / time	1 M.A. / Hr. no. units / time
(c) What is the performance per worker/group/system at the beginning of the HRD program?	1 M.A. / Hr. no. units / time	1 M.A. / Hr. no. units / time	1 M.A. / Hr. no. units / time
(d) What dollar value is assigned to each performance unit?	$ 70 /unit	$ 70 /unit	$ 70 /unit
(e) What is the development time required to reach the expected performance level?	240 Hr. no. time	240 Hr. no. time	56 Hr. no. time
(f) What is the assessment period? (Enter the longest time (e) of all options being considered.)	240 Hr. no. time	24 Hr. no. time	240 Hr. no. time
(g) How many workers/groups/ systems will participate in your HRD program?	25 no. ⟨workers⟩ groups/systems	25 no. ⟨workers⟩ groups/systems	25 no. ⟨workers⟩ groups/systems
Calculations to determine net performance value:			
(h) Usable units worker/group/system produce during the HRD program. If no, enter -0-. If yes, enter known performance rate or calculate average performance rate $[(b + c)/2]$	.5 M.A. no. units	0 M.A. no. units	0 M.A. no. units
(i) What are the total units per worker/ group/system produced during the development time? $(h \times e)$	120 no. of units	0 no. of units	0 no. of units
(j) How many units will be produced per worker/work group system during the assessment period? $\{[(f - e) \times b] + i\}$	120 no. of units	216 no. of units	184 no. of units
(k) What is the value of the worker's/group's/system's performance during the assessment period? $(j \times d)$	$ 8,400	$ 15,120	$ 12,880
(l) What is the performance value gain per worker/group/system? $[k - (c \times d \times f)]$	$ 8,400	$ 15,120	$ 12,880
(m) What is the total performance value gain for all workers/groups/ systems? $(l \times g)$	$ 210,000 (Option 1)	$ 378,000 (Option 2)	$ 322,000 (Option 3)

Note that performance units and time units for all options must remain consistent throughout the assessment.

FIGURE 7.4 Performance Value Worksheet: Service Industry

Program/Intervention _Service Industry - Market Analysis_   Analyst _____ Date _____

Option name	1 _Unstructured_	2 _Vendor_	3 _In-House_
Analyze:			
Performance Diagnosis			
Document Expertise			9,421
Other			
Other			
Design:			
General HRD program design		6,000	
Specific HRD program design		6,800	3,000
Other			
Other			
Develop:			
Draft and prototype			1,000
Pilot test and revise			
Production and duplication			200
Other			
Other			
Implement:			
Program management			300
Program delivery		12,290	580
Participation costs			
Other _("Buddy Salaries")_	5,000		
Other			
Evaluate:			
Results assessment and report		200	200
Performance follow-up			
Other			
Other			
<u>Total HRD costs</u>	$ 5,000	$ 25,290	$ 14,701
	(Option 1)	(Option 2)	(Option 3)

FIGURE 7.5   Cost Worksheet: Service Industry

Program Intervention: <u>Service Industry—Market Analysis</u>

Analyst: _____ Date: _____

Option	1. Unstructured	2. Vendor	3. In-House
Performance Value	$ _210,000_	$ _378,000_	$ _322,000_
Minus Cost	$ _5,000_	$ _25,290_	$ _14,701_
Benefit	$ _205,000_	$ _352,710_	$ _307,299_

Note: Circle your choice of option:

FIGURE 7.6   Benefit Worksheet: Service Industry

Conclusion

If you are ready to dive into the pool, I advise you to back off for a while. I suggest that you *start with an uncontroversial project or consider keeping your first-time-ever forecast to yourself.* Professionals learning any new skill have enough challenges without choosing a difficult project. Later, when you have practiced and gained expertise, apply the HRD financial forecasting method to a controversial or highly visible project in your company. But first try the method out on small, low-risk HRD programs. Develop a feel for the process and learn the analytical thinking skills that are essential to using the financial forecasting model. Don't forget that you are likely to encounter politics related to company financial matters with which you need to become familiar. Becoming an expert takes time.

The rest is up to you. Run away? Dive into the deep end first? Neither are recommended. The suggestion is to simply practice.

8

Actual Financial Benefits—Case Examples

In this chapter two case situations of assessing *actual* financial benefits of human resource development (HRD) will be presented. Figure 1.2, Framework and Key Questions for Assessing HRD Financial Benefits, asks, What is the *actual financial benefit* resulting from an HRD intervention? This is a during-the-process assessment based on actual financial data.

Two cases are presented in this chapter to highlight the fact that the *actual* financial benefit method can be used in a wide variety of situations—in the government and private sectors, for profit and nonprofit enterprises, in manufacturing and service organizations. This method of assessing *actual* financial benefits can be used in any situation where HRD efforts contribute to the achievement of valued organizational goals. The case examples are meant to increase confidence that the financial benefit assessment method works. For each case in this chapter detailed case facts, a critique of the facts, and completed performance value, cost, and benefit worksheets are presented.

Organization Development Case.   Achieving a new level of customer service throughout the health care organization is the crucial aim of HRD in this case. The ultimate goal is to attract and maintain valued members (see Figures 8.1, 8.2, and 8.3).

Management Consulting Case.   A management consulting firm works out its own methods for managing projects. The forecast performance value of a structured HRD program is instructive to decisionmakers (see Figures 8.4, 8.5, and 8.6).

Organization Development Case: Actual Financial Benefit

Situation. Universal Healthcare operates in a very aggressive market. The organization's market research has pointed out that its services are not much different from those of its competitors. They further have stated that there is room for growth in the company's market. As director of HRD you agree with top management's conviction that poor customer service is a serious problem for Universal Healthcare and that an organization development intervention aimed at creating a new "sense of the customer" in employees will result in maintaining current members and attracting new members. Plans include a companywide organization development effort to instill a "sense of the customer" in Universal's employees and a specific customer relations training program for ten salespeople whose goal is to attract new members.

The options were to produce an in-house organization development intervention using Universal's HRD staff or to use a similar off-the-shelf program that is available from an external development firm. Both options would involve participants in several sessions over the next year. The in-house version promised a gain of 1,200 new members in one year's time. The gain from the off-the-shelf program is expected to be 500 in the same time period. The in-house program was selected and actual financial benefits assessed. Healthcare's financial director valued that one new member, after all expenses, leaves Universal Healthcare with $200 net profit. This was a key figure in calculating the value of the added subscribers at year's end.

Critique. This case has four interesting aspects. First, the unit of performance—new members—was easy to identify and difficult to value. Only a few people at the top of the organization knew the dollar value of the annual net profit from each membership. It took probing to finally discover it.

Second, since all employees of the organization participated in the customer-service program, the entire organization was considered to be a single work group. The increase in membership was not an individual worker goal—it was an organizational goal.

Third, the custom-made, in-house option, because it fit the problem so well, proved to be more effective in terms of expected performance at the end of the one-year evaluation period—1,400 members instead of the forecasted 1,200. An extension of this performance picture had to do with the accounting procedures used by Universal Healthcare. A membership sale is based on a business calendar year. Thus, a new member joining at midyear only pays and joins for half a year. This unit is thus a one-half member rather than a full member. Because of this—and because the exact performance rate was not easily accessible and the company traditionally used this conservative approach to handling data—the average membership units during the assessment period were calculated. Seven hundred new members were attributed to the in-house program, 50 percent of the 1,400 new members.

Actual Costs and Benefits. The actual benefits in the organization development case proved to be a sound investment. The HRD intervention cost $24,000 (salaries are not included in such calculations in Universal Healthcare and no additional staff were added) compared to the lower-cost $15,000 option that was not selected. Cost, however, is not an assessment of economic benefit. The higher-cost option yielded so much additional performance value that the cost difference was meaningless. The in-house version significantly altered corporate values as they related to the importance of customers. The program intended to challenge each employee to develop a "sense of the customer," which had been lacking in the organization, and succeeded in terms of bottom-line assessment. Given their competitive situation, the decisionmakers found it too risky to not change the organization's culture. The final benefit of $256,000 was an ROI of 11:1 (performance value of $280,000 divided by the cost of $24,000 is 11.67 to 1 and conservatively reported as 11:1).

The *actual* calculations in this case were astonishing and potentially unbelievable. Three facts made the data believable:

- The financial value of each new member was established by the person with the most financial authority in the organization.

Program/Intervention *Organization Development - Customer Service*	Analyst _____	Date _____
Option name:	1___*In-house*___	2_____

Data required for calculations:		
(a) What unit of performance are you measuring?	*Members (Mbr.)* unit name	_____ unit name
(b) What is the performance goal per worker/group/system at the end of your HRD program?	1400 *Mbr.* / *Yr.* no. units / time	___ ___ / ___ no. units / time
(c) What is the performance per worker/group/system at the beginning of the HRD program?	0 *Mbr.* / *Yr.* no. units / time	___ ___ / ___ no. units / time
(d) What dollar value is assigned to each performance unit?	$ _200_ /unit	$_____ /unit
(e) What is the development time required to reach the expected performance level?	1 *Yr.* no. time	___ ___ no. time
(f) What is the assessment period? (Enter the longest time (e) of all options being considered.)	1 *Yr.* no. time	___ ___ no. time
(g) How many workers/groups/systems will participate in your HRD program?	1 no. workers/groups/systems⟲	_____ no. workers/groups/systems

Calculations to determine net performance value:		
(h) Usable units worker/group/system produce during the HRD program. If no, enter -0-. If yes, enter known performance rate or calculate average performance rate [(b + c)/2]	700 *Mbr.* no. units	___ ___ no. units
(i) What are the total units per worker/group/system produced during the development time? (h x e)	700 no. of units	_____ no. of units
(j) How many units will be produced per worker/work group/system during the assessment period? {[(f – e) x b] + i}	700 no. of units	_____ no. of units
(k) What is the value of the worker's/group's/system's performance during the assessment period? (j x d)	$ _140,000_	$ _____
(l) What is the performance value gain per worker/group/system? [k – (c x d x f)]	$ _140,000_	$ _____
(m) What is the total performance value gain for all workers/groups/systems? (l x g)	$ _140,000_ (Option 1)	$ _____ (Option 2)

Note that performance units and time units for all options <u>must remain consistent</u> throughout the assessment.

FIGURE 8.1   Performance Value Worksheet: Organization Development

114

Program/Intervention _Organization Development - Customer Service_ Analyst _____ Date _____

Option name	1 _In-House_	2 _____
Analyze & Contract		
Analyze	5,000	
Contract	5,000	
Proposal to management	1,000	
Other _____		
Other _____		
Diagnose & Feedback		
Diagnosis	3,500	
Feedback	500	
Other _____		
Other _____		
Plan, Design, & Develop		
Plan	500	
Design	500	
Develop	2,000	
Other _____		
Other _____		
Implement:		
Manage	2,500	
Deliver	2,500	
Other _____		
Other _____		
Evaluate & Institutionalize		
Assess Results	500	
Report Results	500	
Institutionalize		
Other _____		
Total OD costs	$ 24,000	$
	(Option 1)	(Option 2)

FIGURE 8.2   Cost Worksheet: Organization Development

	Organization Development -	Date _____
Program/Intervention	Customer Service	Analyst _____

Option	1 _____ In-House _____	2 _____
Performance Value	$ _____ 280,000 _____	$ _____
Minus Cost	24,000	_____
Benefit	$ (256,000)	$ _____

NOTE: Circle your choice of option.
ROI = 280,000 ÷ 24,000 (11.67:1, or 11:1)

FIGURE 8.3   Benefit Worksheet: Organization Development

- The use of the half-year value of each new member is believed by decisionmakers in the organization to be an underestimate (average membership time period of new members brought the number to 700 instead of 1,400).
- The geographic region involved has systematic, ongoing market share data on all health care providers that showed the increases in subscriptions also represented parallel increases in market share.

Management Development Case: Actual Financial Benefit

Situation.   A division of a large management-consulting firm specializes in the design and installation of information systems for business clients. The systems include computers, computer software, and system know-how. The firm has developed a well-publicized systems approach to which their consultants closely adhere when working with client projects. The system has five major phases and three dozen specific steps.

Four project directors supervise ten to twelve consultants, seeing to it that original contracts are honored and that the "system" of the firm is followed. A performance diagnosis revealed that project directors were experiencing uneven work flow, stalled projects, and projects of uneven quality, which have the long-term potential of affecting the market position of their firm. Simply stated, many of the information system projects were out of control.

The HRD department worked with the four project directors to propose a new project management work system to increase the quality and efficiency of projects. The new work system was to provide an efficient means to monitor, plan, and communicate the design and installation of information systems. The executive vice president of operations and the comptroller determined that strict adherence to the quality features of the firm's "system" and potential gains in efficiency would result in a first-year market share gain of 1 percent, worth $150,000 in net profit.

Critique.   This is an interesting case for several reasons. First, the mere existence of a logical information system does not mean that it is known who does what and when. A seemingly logical system can get out of control or, as in this case, may never have really been under control. Even so, the firm has 41 percent of the market share to show for its information system and good personnel. What is now needed is a good *project management system* to orchestrate client needs, the information system, consultants, and project directors.

Second, without the new project management system, the firm's performance was forecast to remain steady. With a new work method in place, a modest 1 percent increase in market share was forecast by the end of the first year.

A third interesting point is the selection of market share percentage as the unit of performance. The original performance diagnosis focused on day-to-day inefficiencies and the slipping quality features of the information system. This operations information was instrumental in designing the new project management system but was set aside in favor of percent of market share gain when the decision about unit of performance was made. This is a difficult but logical leap. Also, top executives in the firm valued the worth of market share gains.

Management Development. The management case is a classic "go/no-go" situation. The organization's project management problems appear to be of long standing. Staying with the current situation will bring no added performance value, no cost, and no gain. In contrast, the redesigned work system cost $21,000 and brought $150,000 in performance value gain and thus a benefit of $129,000 (Figure 8.6).

The company is not in financial crisis, even though aspects of the current situation are chaotic. For this reason, the decision criteria of appropriateness, quality, and prior effectiveness dominated the decision process in choosing the selected HRD intervention. In the past, new work systems backfired in this organization, so the decisionmakers wanted evidence that the new system would succeed. The business climate remained steady, as anticipated, a 1 percent increase in market share resulted, and beyond this the work feels saner.

The reported ROI was calculated by dividing the $150,000 performance value divided by the $21,000 cost to yield an ROI of just over 7:1. Figures 8.4 and 8.5 show the actual $21,000 cost breakdown and the $150,000 performance values.

Conclusion

Determining *actual* financial benefits is relatively easy given two important conditions. First, you must have identified an important performance goal that requires an HRD intervention. Second, the intervention must be systematically implemented. These two conditions focus on the goal, the outcome, and the means of getting there.

The other two financial benefit methods, *forecasting* (before the fact) and *approximating* (after the fact), are more risky. Here, the job is to simply capture the data. But if an HRD intervention is ill-proposed and poorly implemented, capturing the costs will work but the performance value may not appear.

		1 _Existing Situation_	2 _Project Mgt._
Program/Intervention	_Management Development - Project Management_ **Analyst** _____ **Date** _____		
	Option name:		

Data required for calculations:

	1 _Existing Situation_	2 _Project Mgt._
(a) What unit of performance are you measuring?	_Percent Market Share (M.S.)_ unit name	_Percent Market Share (M.S.)_ unit name
(b) What is the performance goal per worker/group/system at the end of your HRD program?	_41_ _M.S._ / _Yr._ no. units / time	_42_ _M.S._ / _Yr._ no. units / time
(c) What is the performance per worker/group/system at the beginning of the HRD program?	_41_ _M.S._ / _Yr._ no. units / time	_41_ _M.S._ / _Yr._ no. units / time
(d) What dollar value is assigned to each performance unit?	$ _150,000_ /unit	$ _150,000_ /unit
(e) What is the development time required to reach the expected performance level?	_1_ _Yr._ no. time	_1_ _Yr._ no. time
(f) What is the assessment period? (Enter the longest time (e) of all options being considered.)	_1_ _Yr._ no. time	_1_ _Yr._ no. time
(g) How many workers/groups/systems will participate in your HRD program?	_1_ no. workers/ groups	_1_ no. workers/ groups

Calculations to determine net performance value:

(h) Usable units worker/group/system produce during the HRD program? If no, enter -0-. If yes, enter known performance rate or calculate average performance rate [$(b + c)/2$]	_41_ _M.S._ no. units	_42_ _M.S._ no. units
(i) What are the total units per worker/group/system produced during the development time? (h x e)	_41_ no. of units	_42_ no. of units
(j) How many units produced per worker/work group/system during the assessment period? $\{[(f - e) \times b] + i\}$	_41_ no. of units	_42_ no. of units
(k) What is the value of the worker's/group's/system's performance during the assessment period? (j x d)	$ _6,300,000_	$ _6,300,000_
(l) What is the performance value gain per worker/group/system? [$k - (c \times d \times f)$]	$ _0_	$ _150,000_
(m) What is the total performance value gain for all workers/groups/systems? (l x g)	$ _0_ (Option 1)	$ _150,000_ (Option 2)

Note that performance units and time units for all options <u>must remain consistent</u> throughout the assessment.

FIGURE 8.4   Performance Value Worksheet: Management Development

Program/Intervention *Management Development - Project Management* Analyst _____ Date _____

Option name	1 *Existing Situation*	2 *Project Mgt.*
Analyze:		
Performance Diagnosis		2,000
Work analysis		2,000
Proposal to management		500
Other _____		
Other _____		
Design:		
General program design		500
Specific program design		1,000
Other *(consultant review)*		1,000
Other _____		
Develop:		
Draft and prototype		2,000
Pilot test and revise		4,000
Production and duplication		500
Other _____		
Other _____		
Implement:		
Program management		1,000
Program delivery		5,000
Participant costs		
Other _____		
Other _____		
Evaluation:		
Program assessment and report		500
Performance follow-up		1,000
Other _____		
Other _____		
Total T&D costs	$ _____	$ 21,000
	(Option 1)	(Option 2)

FIGURE 8.5   Cost Worksheet: Management Development

Program/Intervention _Management Development -
Project Management_   Date _____
Analyst _____

Option	1 _Existing Situation_	2 _Project Mgt._
Performance Value	$ _____ 0 _____	$ _____ 150,000 _____
Minus Cost	_____ 0 _____	_____ 21,000 _____
Benefit	$ _____ 0 _____	$ _____ 129,000 _____

NOTE: Circle your choice of option.

FIGURE 8.6   Benefit Worksheet: Management Development

Calculating *actual* financial benefits is the least controversial financial benefit method. Even so, very few HRD interventions are financially assessed. Given the easy potential to demonstrate high returns on investments, it seems like a foolish state of affairs.

Approximated Financial Benefits—Case Examples

In this chapter two case situations of assessing *approximated* financial benefits of human resource development (HRD) will be presented. Figure 1.2, Framework and Key Questions for Assessing HRD Financial Benefits, asks, What is the *approximate* financial benefit resulting from an HRD intervention? This is an after-the-fact assessment based on approximated financial data.

Two cases are presented in this chapter to highlight the fact that the *approximate* financial benefit method can be used in a wide variety of situations—in the government and private sectors, for profit and nonprofit enterprises, and in manufacturing and service organizations. This method of assessing *approximate* financial benefits can be used in any situation where HRD efforts are believed to contribute to the achievement of valued organizational goals. For each case in this chapter we present detailed case facts and analysis. The case examples are intended to increase confidence that the financial benefit assessment method works.

FIGURE 9.1 Model of the Critical Outcome Technique

Sales Communication Case. This case illustrates the use of the critical outcome technique (Swanson and Mattson, 1997) as an essential strategy for *approximating* the performance value resulting from a sales communication intervention in a major insurance company (see Figure 9.1). Since determining the performance value is the most illusive task, having a simple tool like the critical outcome technique is invaluable in approximating the performance value of an intervention. As usual, the cost side of the assessment of financial benefit is relatively easy. In this case the intervention was purchased from an external provider at a fixed cost and there were some added internal costs that could be tracked down from expenditure records. The benefits are simply a subtraction of the approximate performance value minus the cost (real or approximate) to yield the approximate benefit (see Figures 9.2, 9.3, 9.4).

Public Sector Case. This case illustrates use of the *approximation* method in a government setting. The HRD program goal is to develop coaching skills in experienced staff so that new staff can more rapidly reach skilled performance in the field.

Sales Communication Case: Approximate Financial Benefits

Situation. A major insurance company was experiencing losses of sales in big accounts. The sales training and performance consulting department became involved and moved quickly. The goal was to increase sales and they jumped right in. Even though they took a systematic approach, they did not think seriously about the financial assessment until the intervention was delivered across the nation. Although the program was expensive in traditional HRD terms, individual sales were huge. However, it took only a handful of sales to fulfill a salesperson's annual sales quota, so the loss of a few of these huge sales from each salesperson could threaten the company division.

The essential development strategy was to figure out what was going wrong, to create a new sales closing process that engaged salespeople and sales managers in a new relationship, and then to train all parties with directly connected on-the-job performance appraisals. The essential strategy for *approximating* the financial benefit of the sales communica-

Program/Intervention   Sales Communication _____   **Analyst** _____   **Date** _____

	Option name:	1 __T&D+OD____	2_____

Data required for calculations:

		Option 1	Option 2
(a)	What unit of performance are you measuring?	___Account Sale___ unit name	_____ unit name
(b)	What is the performance goal per worker/group/system at the end of your HRD program?	___ _A.S._ /___ no. units / time	___ _____ /___ no. units / time
(c)	What is the performance per worker/group/system at the beginning of the HRD program?	___ _____ /___ no. units / time	___ _____ /___ no. units / time
(d)	What dollar value is assigned to each performance unit?	$_____/unit	$_____/unit
(e)	What is the development time required to reach the expected performance level?	_____ _____ no. time	_____ _____ no. time
(f)	What is the assessment period? (Enter the longest time (e) of all options being considered.)	__9__ _month_ no. time	_____ _____ no. time
(g)	How many workers/groups/systems will participate in your HRD program?	180 workers/system no. workers/groups/ (systems)	_____ no. workers/groups/ systems

Calculations to determine net performance value:

		Option 1	Option 2
(h)	Useable units workers/groups/systems produce during the HRD program? If no, enter -0-. If yes, enter known performance rate or calculate average performance rate [$(b + c)/2$]	_____ _____ no. units	_____ _____ no. units
(i)	What are the total units per worker/group/system produced during the development time? ($h \times e$)	_____ no. of units	_____ no. of units
(j)	How many units are there produced per worker/work group/(system) during the assessment period? $\{[(f - e) \times b] + i\}$	____24____ no. of units	_____ no. of units
(k)	What is the value of the worker's/group's/(system's) performance during the assessment period? ($j \times d$)	$ _8,410,000*_	$ _____
(l)	What is the performance value gain per worker/group/system? [$k - (c \times d \times f)$]	$ _8,410,000*_	$ _____
(m)	What is the total performance value gain for all workers/groups/(systems) ($l \times g$)	$ _8,410,000*_ (Option 1)	$ _____ (Option 2)

*Note: The actual 24 sales attributed to the sales communication program were able to be financially valued by the company comptroller

FIGURE 9.2   Performance Value Worksheet: Sales Communication

Program/Intervention <u>Sales Communication</u> Analyst _____ Date _____

Option Name 1 <u> T&D + OD </u> 2 _____

	Option 1	Option 2
Analyze		
Step 1	15,000	
Step 2	10,000	
Step 3		
Step 4		
Propose		
Step 1	5,000	
Step 2		
Step 3		
Step 4		
Create		
Step 1	50,000	
Step 2		
Step 3		
Step 4		
Implement		
Step 1	50,000	
Step 2	60,000	
Step 3	80,000	
Step 4		
Assess		
Step 1	15,000	
Step 2	3,000	
Step 3		
Step 4		
Total HRD costs	$ 288,000	$
	288,000	(Option 2)

FIGURE 9.3   Cost Worksheet: Sales Communication

Date_____

Program/Intervention _Sales Communication_____

Analyst_____

Option	1	_T&D + HRD_	2	
Performance Value	$	8,410,000	$	
Minus Cost		288,000		
Benefit	$	8,122,000	$	

FIGURE 9.4   Benefit Worksheet: Sales Communication

tion intervention was to go back and gather the costs—easy enough, given the company's accounting system—and then attempt to approximate any new sales attributable to the sales communication intervention. Once this was approximated using the critical outcome technique, described in Chapter 2, benefits could be calculated like the *forecasted* and *actual* financial assessment methods.

The inquiry question in this instance was very simple and direct. It was an extension of the outcome definition: *The intended outcome was to an increase in sales resulting from improved communication.* The outcome inquiry, in the form of an e-mail sent to every participant, asked the question: *Did you make any sales that you may not have otherwise made as a result of your participation in the sales communication program? If yes, please list all those sales and their value.* Using the technique, all reported sales would need to be verified through organization records and/or supervisory confirmation.

In this case the purpose of the program of making sales and the means of documenting sales was clear and workable. Approximating financial benefits using the critical outcome technique can also be applied to more general interventions. For example, general communication training (not specialized and targeted sales communication training) and general supervisory and management development could result in a va-

COT Outcome Inquiry Tool
Critical Outcome Technique

Program Title: Coaching 101
Program date(s): April 12–15, xxxx

Corporate Training & Development is interested in understanding how you have been able to take what you learned in the coaching 101 program and put it intopractice back on the job. We would appreciate itif you would take a few minutes to complete the survey; your responses will help us imrpove this program for future participants, Thank you for your time.

Some of the questions in this survey require that you think about what you have been able to implement from the coaching 101 program, while other questions require that you think about the results of the implementation. The diagram below illustrates an example of potential skill or learning applications and the potential results or outcomes.

Used the performance development planning tool to provide targeted feedback to my direct reports on a weekly basis.	*Noticed a decrease in call handling time in three of my direct reports as a result of their using my feedback to develop their performance.*

Please read each of the Learning Application Statements below and check the box which best represents the frequency of application of the Coaching 101 program learnings

0 = not applicalbe/have not applied this
1 = once per month or less
2 = a few times per month
3 = once a week
4 = a few times a week
5 = every day

	1	2	3	4	5
Provide specific performance-related feedback to my direct reports.	☐	☐	☐	☐	☐
Gain a clear understanding of the problem(s) to be addressed.	☐	☐	☐	☐	☐
Give feedback in the appropriate setting.	☐	☐	☐	☐	☐
Use the 'opening up' technique to get employees to offer self-rating.	☐	☐	☐	☐	☐
Check if employees understood the feedback and the importance of the situation	☐	☐	☐	☐	☐
Create a mutual action plan with the employee.	☐	☐	☐	☐	☐
Follow up with the employee at the appropriate interval to ensure completion.	☐	☐	☐	☐	☐

I have seen the following as a result of my application of the learnings of the Coaching 101 program (please check the appropriate results and provide a brief description.):

Turnover:

☐ I retained an employee(s) I was expecting to terminate or demote: _____

Staff Productivity:

☐ Call Handling Time: _____

☐ Service Level Improvement: _____

☐ Number of Escalated Calls: _____

☐ Customer Complaints: _____

☐ Cross-selling: _____

☐ Other: _____

FIGURE 9.5   Sample Outcome Inquiry Tool for Less Focused Intervention

source: B.W. Mattson (2000). Reprinted with permission.

riety of outcomes, not just one kind of outcome like a sale in the previous example. In these instances the development of the outcome inquiry takes more thought and planning. An example is shown in Figure 9.5. This outcome inquiry tool sent to participants after the fact attempts to identify a variety of potential mission-related units of performance that could result from managers taking a general program in *coaching skills.* Each one of any type of reported and verified outcomes could be financially valued (for example, reduction in customer complaints, heading off an employee expected to quit, and so forth).

Critique. This case is unique for a number of reasons. There are few performance units (large single sales) per salesperson, and each is worth a great deal. It takes salespeople extensive time to build a relationship with the customer and to close a sale. Furthermore, salespeople were hesitant to give anybody but themselves credit for accomplishments. How, then, could a sale result from the sales communication intervention? The HRD intervention was expensive, yet the income from a single sale would more than pay for the intervention, which focused on the sales force of more than 150 people. In approximating the actual sales attributable to the intervention a period of six months was covered (less than adequate) and the assumption was that it would be incomplete (an underestimate). Even so, $4,590,000 in sales were reported and attributed to HRD.

Costs and Benefits. The *approximated* costs and benefits of this case yielded a 7:1 ROI for the six-month assessment period. Much cheaper sales training that proceeded this business-focused effort was thought to be outrageously expensive, and the new $610,000 intervention cost much more. Even so, the sales communication programs ended up being inexpensive and a good investment, given the *approximated* benefits (see Figure 9.4).

Public Sector Case: Approximate Financial Benefits

Situation. The HRD manager of a public-sector auditing and collection agency regularly put groups of new recruits through a 240-hour training course before sending them off to work in the field. The course was, however, just the beginning of their training. On average, an additional fifteen months were required for new staff to become competent. Believing that the time to reach full performance could be shortened, the training manager gathered a committee of eight experts to discuss the situation and to devise a plan for accelerating learning on the job. Their strategy was simple: teach experienced staff how to more effectively coach new staff. After exploring several alternative packages for teaching coaching skills, the committee settled on the option of asking the National Association of Auditors to conduct a four-day training program. This option was compared to the current, more leisurely method of gaining full competency. Ten experienced staff who generally coached one new worker were trained. After the program had been implemented, management asked the training manager to conduct a cost-benefit analysis of the project and to include the committee's work in the project's costs. (see Figures 9.6 and 9.7).

Critique. *Approximating* performance impact was tricky. An auditor-collector works with a number of clients who have extremely diverse characteristics. Thus, one client's work could take many days to process, whereas another's could be processed in a few hours. Clients' personalities and the variety of their economic endeavors confound the issue of finding an appropriate unit of work performance. *Approximating* the impact of the coaching on the efficient completion of specific cases was left to each auditor. Only cases verified by supervisors as being truly the result of the coaching intervention were retained as units of performance to be entered into the calculations. Establishing the value of the unit of performance—dollars of collections per hour and a performance standard of $175 of collections per hour—required a consensus decision on the part of several top managers. This average accommodated all the types and sizes of clients that any one auditor-collector could be expected to work with over a period of time.

Costs and Benefits. The public sector case described an auditing and collection agency whose new staff had previously required fifteen months of field experience to reach competency. A program to teach coaching skills to experienced staff for use when working with new staff was determined to be an appropriate method for shortening the process of developing new staff. The assessor looked at two options—the existing fifteen-month development program and a new thirteen-month structured option. The approximate (after-the-fact) financial benefit assessment was favorable for HRD—$280,000 minus $47,415—$232,585 in benefit. Again, this is based on partial data of units of performance attributable to the HRD intervention and verified by the supervisor.

Conclusion

There is a real place for assessing the financial benefit of HRD interventions using the *approximation* method. This method is potentially the lowest-cost and highest-gain method of the three presented. Given available cost data and credible estimates of performance outcomes, even the most anemic HRD programs will almost always yield a greater benefit than cost. That would be good results data for any HRD practitioner to be able to report.

Program/Intervention _Public Sector - Coaching Skills_ **Analyst** _____ **Date** _____

		Existing Situation	
Option name:	1	_Unstructured_	2 _NAA Course_

Data required for calculations:		
(a) What unit of performance are you measuring?	_____ unit name	_Audit_ unit name
(b) What is the performance goal per worker/group/system at the end of your HRD program?	___ ___ / ___ no. units / time	_1.0_ _Audit_ / _Hr._ no. units / time
(c) What is the performance per worker/group/system at the beginning of the HRD program?	___ ___ / ___ no. units / time	_0_ _$_ / _Hr._ no. units / time
(d) What dollar value is assigned to each performance unit?	$_____ /unit	$ _175_ /unit
(e) What is the development time required to reach the expected performance level?	___ ___ no. time	___ ___ no. time
(f) What is the assessment period? (Enter the longest time (e) of all options being considered.)	___ ___ no. time	_160_ _Hrs._ no. time
(g) How many workers/groups/systems will participate in your HRD program?	_____ no. workers/ groups/systems	_10_ no. ⟨workers⟩ groups/systems

Calculations to determine net performance value:		
(h) Usable units worker/group/system produce during the HRD program? If no, enter -0-. If yes, enter known performance rate or calculate average performance rate $[(b + c)/2]$	___ ___ no. units	_87_ _Audit_ no. units
(i) What are the total units per worker/group/system produced during the development time? $(h \times e)$	_____ no. of units	_____ no. of units
(j) How many units will be produced per worker/work group/system during the assessment period? $\{[(f - e) \times b] + i\}$	_____ no. of units	_160_ no. of units
(k) What is the value of the worker's/group's/system's performance during the assessment period? $(j \times d)$	$ _____	$ _28,000_
(l) What is the performance value gain per worker/group/system? $[k - (c \times d \times f)]$	$ _____	$ _28,000_
(m) What is the total performance value gain for all workers/groups/systems? $(l \times g)$	$ _____ (Option 1)	$ _280,000_ (Option 2)

Note that performance units and time units for all options <u>must remain consistent</u> throughout the assessment.

FIGURE 9.6 Performance Value Worksheet: Public Sector

Program/Intervention _Public Sector -_
Coaching Skills _____ Analyst _____ Date _____

Option name	1 _Existing Situation Unstructured_	2 _NAA Course_
Analyze:		
Performance Diagnosis		3,296
Work analysis		
Proposal to management		70
Other _(tuition and time)_		680
Other _____		
Design:		
Program design		412
Other _____		
Other _____		
Develop:		
Draft and prototype		
Pilot test and revise		
Production and duplication		280
Other _(HRD manager)_		82
Implement:		
Program management		
Program delivery		3,000
Participant costs		38,400
Other _(HRD manager)_		164
Evaluate:		
Program evaluation and report		989
Performance follow-up		
Other _(secretarial)_		42
Other _____		
Total costs _____	$ _____	$ 47,415
	(Option 1)	(Option 2)

FIGURE 9.7   Cost Worksheet: Public Sector

Presenting Financial Benefit Data to Management

This chapter focuses on presenting financial benefit assessments of HRD investments to organizational decision makers and summarizes the model and methods covered in this book. As you already know, calculating the benefit of an HRD program is easy. Simply subtract the cost of the HRD program from the performance value. The balance is the financial benefit. Learning how to present your financial assessment and how to moderate your presentation to accommodate the concerns of decision makers is another matter.

Decisions Based on Finances

With your numbers in hand, decision makers can choose among all options under consideration. This is a fairly straightforward task. They simply choose the option that has the greatest financial benefit, forecasted, actual, or approximated. But wait just a minute! The following advice could help HRD professionals and organizational decision makers maintain perspective.

Wild Figures. Many HRD managers are afraid that they will come up with a crazy, inaccurate assessment. It is important to note that the correctness of the *decision,* not the accuracy of the figures, is what counts. Granted, accuracy of the figures and correctness of the decision are related, but there remains some leeway for the assessor. If all calculations could be accurate to the penny, decisions would be easy. Although this ideal state is not to be found in the real world, research has demonstrated that imperfect numbers are less of a threat to making correct decisions than you might think.

How can this be? The reason is simple. Through many studies it has been found that it is reasonable to rely on the internal consistency of individual assessors. This is particularly reassuring when the *forecasting* method is used. Conservative analysts consistently calculate low benefits for the options they assess. Liberal analysts consistently calculate high benefits for the options they consider. The relative consistency, not the precision, of each analyst's figures is the key. For the same proposed HRD intervention, three analysts may find different benefits figures and still arrive at the same decision as to what option to support. The following example illustrates internal consistency and how the decision maker can have a high level of confidence in making the correct decision, even when given a variety of financial benefit calculations. Two analysts prepared the following forecasted benefits for three HRD options:

	Option 1 Benefit	Option 2 Benefit	Option 3 Benefit
Analyst A	$70,000	$150,000	$170,000
Analyst B	$50,000	$100,000	$125,000

The benefit figures from either assessor will lead decision makers to choose Option 3.

Besides the essential rightness of such decisions, there is an important caution: The acceptance of some variability in benefit figures should not lead you to think that the process condones casual inventions of costs and performance value figures. It was clear that the analysts in the research studies gathered their figures with serious intent and made their calculations with care. This serious approach to the task ensures the internal consistency of the figures developed by each analyst.

Unstructured HRD.   The issue of the relative accuracy of calculated figures is important to organizational strategists and planners who want answers to the following questions:

- How can we assure the greatest return on our available capital?
- Given various options, which one will we choose?

In earlier chapters it was noted that there is no such thing as no HRD. People need to learn their jobs and to structure their systems to achieve their goals. They will do this through trial-and-error means or through more systematic interventions. HRD interventions are meant to enhance the organization's capabilities for reaching planned goals. Most managers believe that they are already effectively enhancing the capabilities of people in their firms. But experience has shown that the most inept managers most likely use the zero-cost, trial-and-error programs. They justify themselves by saying, "Our people develop on the job." These managers little realize their HRD programs' effects, or the lack of them, on workers and on the company's ability to compete in the marketplace. I call this trial-and-error approach to the problem of development *unstructured* HRD (Swanson and Sawzin, 1975), or the unplanned process for developing and unleashing human expertise through accident, acts of God, and the goodwill of employees.

Whenever and wherever unstructured HRD exists in an organization, it is *essential* to gather baseline figures so that unstructured HRD can be compared with forecasted, actual, or approximated results of structured programs. Revealing the financial benefits figures of existing, unstructured HRD will help answer the question, Which is the best HRD option? (By convention, the ongoing unstructured option data is placed in the first column of each worksheet.)

Nonfinancial Criteria

This book has focused on the financial benefits of investing in HRD because this is where there is a general lack of expertise in the HRD profession. This missing expertise in assessing the financial benefits of HRD interventions is a major block to making good organizational investments in HRD and being credited for enhancing the financial performance of the organization. Even without this financial assessment expertise, HRD professionals have been doing quite well. Obviously, criteria other than financial data are being used for choosing HRD interventions from among the available options.

Here are six criteria to use when comparing and choosing among HRD options:

- *Appropriateness* to the organizational culture and tradition
- *Availability* of the intervention
- Perceived *design quality* of the intervention
- *Prior effectiveness* of the same or a similar intervention
- *Cost* of the intervention
- *Financial benefit* to the organization

Financial benefit is only one criteria for choosing a particular option. Then, too, decision makers may not use all six criteria for making every HRD program decision, nor will they always weight each criterion equally.

Assessing costs has been done primarily as a means to calculate the benefits of HRD investments. However, many organizations have a limited amount of available working capital and staying within a limited budget may be mandatory, no matter what the expected benefit of a structured HRD program is. To propose that decision makers invest in HRD programs that are beyond current organizational resources is a lot like asking a poor man with $10 to his name to invest $10,000 on the premise of becoming a millionaire. His reach toward his fortune may begin with a $10 investment—and no more.

The first two criteria listed above—*appropriateness* and *availability*—depend on the context in which they are applied. Applying a criterion of appropriateness to the organizational culture and tradition helps the HRD professional think about alternative HRD interventions in terms of how well they fit. Clearly, interventions that would fail in one organization might succeed in another. Such variables as appropriateness of content, method, facilitator, and location must be taken into consideration.

The second criterion, *availability*, is primarily a question of logistics. Key personnel, dates, time of day, and locations for intervention implementation are often either critical or mandated. If an option is not available when needed, clearly it must be dropped from consideration.

The two quality criteria of *design quality* and *prior effectiveness* of the program also aid in valuing the options being considered. The design criterion is used to evaluate the general strategy and the major elements of the intervention, as well as its potential for meeting the original, carefully defined performance goal. Unfortunately, it is too often simply assumed (without checking) that this criterion has been met. Among an array of options, some designs are more likely to meet the performance goal than others.

To satisfy the second quality criterion, *effectiveness*, the HRD professional must deliberately seek evidence of the prior effectiveness of the same or similar development efforts delivered by the providers of the options under consideration.

Figure 10.1 demonstrates the usefulness of listing decision criteria on one axis and the HRD options under consideration on the other. In this sample decision matrix the six criteria are equally weighted for Options A through D. Each option is rated from 1 (best) to 4 (worst) on each of the selection criteria. The *lowest* score indicates best choice. According to our example, Option B is the one to choose. Taking the same situation and increasing the importance of some of the criteria by weighting them would result in other preferred options.

The ultimate choice will come from a combination of the facts, the intuition of decision makers, and their willingness to take risks. Making your own choice among the available options is another thing. In the remainder of this chapter, I discuss presenting proposals and reports to management.

Figure 10.1   HRD Selection Decision Matrix.

Decision Criteria	HRD Program Options			
	A	B	C	D
1. Appropriateness to culture and tradition	3	2	4	1
2. Availability (date/time/place)	1	2	4	3
3. Quality: Program design	1	2	3	4
4. Quality: Prior effectiveness	2	1	3	4
5. Financial: Benefit	4	1	2	3
6. Financial: Cost	4	3	1	2
Totals	15	11	17	17

NOTE: Rank each option on each criteria: 1 = highest, 4 = lowest.

Presenting Assessment Data to Management

The purpose of this section is to help in gaining management's acceptance of HRD assessments. Assume that a proposed intervention is meant to respond to a carefully determined performance goal and that it is appropriate to the organization's culture. Unless it is designed to meet these two criteria, you will have little, if any, ammunition with which to defend it against its critics or against other, non-HRD options. In addition, a skillful presentation of the program proposal to management is essential.

At a minimum, most HRD reports contain five major elements:

- Performance requirement
- Intervention goal
- Intervention options
- Recommended action
- Assessment (forecasted, actual, approximate)

Performance Requirement. The performance requirement is a carefully determined and desired change in organizational, work group, or individual contributor performance. The need can be expressed in the form of a performance goal or a performance deficiency, either of which should be central to the mission of the organization.

Intervention Goal. Both HRD and non-HRD factors will probably influence progress toward the performance goal in question. Changing the required system is an example of a non-HRD program that could be instituted along with an HRD program. Whenever a parallel non-HRD program will be instituted to cope with the same performance goal, the HRD program goal will typically be smaller in scope than the identified organizational goal or the total performance deficiency. Adjusting HRD program goals to the realities of the situation is critical to establish long-term credibility for HRD. Promising outcomes that cannot be delivered will only cause problems for the HRD department down the road. So promise what you know you can deliver and on occasion, surprise yourself and management with more than you promised.

Intervention (Options).   The third element involves presentation of the HRD program (options). The purpose of this element is to allow decision makers to understand what was done or to choose the single best HRD program option.

(Recommended) Action.   The fourth element is to summarize the action taken to management to critique or to recommend the action. This is where you must stand on your own two feet. You may need to make a persuasive argument; you are also prepared for criticism and possible rejection.

Remember that a sound performance diagnosis is essential if genuine performance requirements and the strategic performance goals of your organization are to be identified. Important performance needs and goals are the basis for responsible HRD programs and for sound financial forecasting of program benefits. Consult Rummler and Brache (1995) and Swanson (1996) for advice on conducting performance diagnoses. You should also understand that there are both good and bad upfront assessments. Good assessments are not necessarily lengthy or complicated. Unfortunately, too many HRD experts would lead you to believe that this is the case.

Assessment (forecasted, actual, approximate).   Here is where the assessment of the financial benefit fits into the picture. When this data is in harmony and supports the first four points, the likelihood for support is greatly enhanced.

Presenting Proposal to Management

It should not be a surprise that up-front proposals and after-the-fact reports have common elements. At a minimum, most HRD reports succinctly repeat the five major elements that appeared in the original proposals given to the organization for approval. They were:

- Performance requirement
- Intervention goal
- Intervention options
- Recommended action
- Assessment (forecasted, actual, approximate)

Thus, the date of the original proposal will reappear in the report. Do not assume that the recipient of the report will have or remember the original proposal. The additional key points in this reporting effort are to highlight the *actual* or *approximated* financial results. Noting baseline data and the conservative nature of the financial figures cited in the report could further enhance the results.

It is also very effective to insert one or two quotes from respected people in the organization who had firsthand experience with the intervention. A quote like this can add additional credibility: "We already see that the team-building program has positively impacted on our department's productivity"—Helen Jones.

The last bit of advice relating to HRD financial results reporting is to systematically determine who should receive such reports and have them delivered, whether they ask for them or not. Receiving regular reports of financial benefits from HRD interventions will fundamentally change the perception of HRD by the recipients.

Rules for Presenting Proposals and Reports

Advice for preparing HRD proposals and reports for presentation has been kept to a minimum. Here are four short rules for the presentation itself:

- Keep it simple.
- Present visual and verbal information in your proposal.
- Talk to the person(s) with authority.
- Strive for believability.

Because presentation situations vary, the above rules are not listed in the order of their importance. Consider the circumstances of a particular presentation and order the rules accordingly.

Keep It Simple.   Simplicity is both beautiful and illusive. Most of us take pleasure in hearing important thoughts presented concisely, clearly, and with their fullness intact. Most of us know when we see or hear elegant simplicity, yet we have to struggle to achieve elegant simplicity in our own efforts. Simple ideas—right or wrong—are generally more acceptable to people than complex ideas. But keeping your presentation simple without losing the integrity of the idea is the hard part. In the short run, complexity will be the easier path to take. In the long run, making the extra effort to achieve simplicity will provide a larger payoff.

Because simplicity is one of the strengths of the HRD benefit-assessment method, be careful not to lose this simplicity at the proposal stage. I know HRD managers who cannot resist telling everything they know when they present their proposals to management. They seem to think that reporting all their hard work will gain them the approval they seek. What it will gain them is a sympathy vote. People in the fund-raising business talk about getting "go-away money." You want more than that. This book has provided you with a simple model and a simple framework for your proposal and reports. Do not abandon elegant simplicity for confusing complexity when you make your presentation to management.

The twin aspects of your presentation are the HRD benefit-assessment model (performance value minus cost equals benefit) and the HRD program reporting (performance requirement, goal, intervention options, program recommendations, and assessment). All these aspects of your presentation should be anchored in the performance issue you have chosen to address, since performance is essential to achieve the fundamental business goals of your company. This kind of approach will lead to your receiving acceptance for your HRD proposals and assessments.

Visual and Verbal.   The saying that "a picture is worth a thousand words" certainly holds true for visually oriented people. For the nonvisual, a picture may be worth less than this, but it will always be worth something. In any organization, some people in management will be verbal, some visual, and some both. The point is that you seek approval from a variety of types of people. Why gamble? Use both verbal and visual symbols when you present your proposal. And, yes, keep them simple.

To the visual and verbal aspects specified above, consider the following: Should you present your reports in person or in the form of written reports, or should you use both methods? Should you present the majority of your ideas through the written word, through graphic illustrations, or both?

As a seeker of management approval and acceptance, you have every-thing to gain by helping decision makers understand what it is that you are reporting. What good does it do to explain at some later time, "I put all that information in the report—if only they had read it"? The neces-sity for communicating in so many dimensions causes outsiders to shudder at the difficulties of business communication. But such is the task. HRD reports and proposals should elicit from management a com-mon vision of HRD. The presentation strategies are as follows:

1. Address each of the five simple report elements.
2. Use the financial benefit assessment method.
3. In making a written report, use concise sentences and paragraphs.
4. Appear in person: Present your information in the same order as your on-paper report and at a pace preferred by your audience.
5. Use one or two visual aids, such as the time-performance graph or the assessment figures, to illustrate the benefit from the intervention. These visuals can be sketched on napkins if you present your proposal over a cup of coffee in the cafeteria or on transparencies if you present in the boardroom.
6. In your written report include the visuals cited above and consider adding other easily understood graphic information, such as performance charts showing sales production, turnover, absenteeism, scrap, and rework.

Authority. If necessary, approach the appropriate decision maker with your report. Of course, it is assumed that you will respect the need to go through channels and to attend to corporate etiquette. Who has the au-thority to make the decision that you seek and who cares about the strategic business need that you propose to address with an HRD pro-gram? It is important to build business alliances with people you contact on the way to reaching the decision maker from whom you need ap-proval. Of course, by giving such advice, you are taking even more risks.

Non–risk takers are easy to spot. In most organizations you hear bitter stories about their having had the same idea for which someone else is getting credit. An unpresented proposal or report is a nonreport. An unreported benefit is a nonbenefit. A report presented by someone who is unfamiliar with it or who is not committed to its content will surely be watered down or relegated to the nearest pile of documents "on hold"— make the presentation yourself and to the right people.

Believability.   The most important piece of advice concerns the relative believability of your report. Given top management's inclination to pressure HRD to contribute more to the organization while it simultaneously shows little confidence in HRD's capacity to do so creates an interesting paradox. An assessment of the true financial benefits to be obtained from a proposed program may exceed top management's willingness to believe that calculation for any number of reasons. Top managers want to work in partnership with HRD, just as they do with other organizational functions. But when managers have more alternatives before them then they can approve, believability becomes an issue. Thus, any facts in your presentation that clearly fall outside the realm of reason or the experience of the decisionmakers will be ignored or discounted. decisionmakers will tend to assume that you are lying to them or trying to trick them. Our advice is to consider working within a "window of believability." What do you suppose will happen if you come along and say, "We can net an 800 percent return on investment in six months." Will the decisionmakers believe you? What is the minimum return on investment that will gain their support? What is the maximum return on investment they will consider feasible? Let's say your group of decisionmakers believes that their investment in HRD could be a break-even proposition and that the maximum potential yield is $2.50 for every $1 invested. What will you do if your most conservative financial benefit forecast is in the neighborhood of $8 for every $1 invested? HRD consultants who use the benefit-assessment method tell us that a proposed return on investment of "at least 2 to 1" will probably be quite attractive and far more acceptable. One general recommendation is to establish a practice of promising at least a 2 to 1 return on investment in forecasting and to compare results of the actual and approximated financial benefits to the same standard. Because the HRD's actual return-on-investment track record has been much better than $2 for every $1 invested in HRD, it feels quite safe in presenting its proposals to management. Believability is an important consideration in gaining approval.

Conclusion

The purpose of this chapter was to develop an understanding of the challenges of presenting HRD proposals and reports to management. Beyond *the* basic financial assessment model, which yields the financial benefit, alternative ways of expressing the benefit have been offered:

- Positive benefit for each option under consideration
- Relative benefit among options
- Return on investment for each option

Two bases for choosing the best HRD program option have been discussed:

- Financial
- Nonfinancial

The purpose of presenting proposals to management is to gain approval for them, and the five elements of a proposal and the final report are:

- Performance requirement
- Intervention goal
- Intervention options
- Recommended action
- Assessment (forecasted, actual, approximate)

Finally, in presenting proposals and reports, keep them simple, use both visual and verbal methods, seek out people in the organization who have real authority, and make sure that your figures are believable.

There are HRD managers who at this point run away from the opportunity to make greater contributions to their organizations. There are those who jump headfirst into the deepest part of the pool. Both responses represent overreactions to new information. Practice must come before confidence. If you are considering the "run-away" response, we offer the following observation: *Do not underestimate the power of this simple assessment tool for communicating with management and thus gaining their approval for responsible HRD programs.*

It is important to understand the relationship between what you do and the benefits you produce. Do not underestimate the importance of knowing your value to your company. The financial benefits model can help you identify worthy activities and support options with the greatest benefit, and you can then go on to develop HRD interventions with confidence in their worth to your organization and ultimately reporting back the actual financial benefits.

Appendix A:

Everything Important in Business and Industry Is Evaluated

The business environment and culture dictate expectations for economic impact of training that must be understood by evaluators.

Richard A. Swanson
University of Minnesota

The mission and goal of business and industry are to maximize the economic return on investment through the production and sale of goods and services. The milieu in which this activity takes place is complex and fluid. The "business" of the private sector is no easy matter. The vulnerability of individual employees, departments, and the organization itself goes beyond the day-to-day experience of most people who work in and with the public sector.

It is in the private sector context of competitiveness and change that business decisionmakers must operate. In contrast, most program evaluation experts have a public sector orientation.

Recently, in my home state of Minnesota, Pillsbury Company was purchased by a British firm, and Control Data Corporation laid off thirty-five

Reprinted with permission: *Evaluating Training Programs in Business and Industry*. New Directions for Program Evaluation, no. 44 (1989), Jossey-Bass.

hundred workers in St. Paul. Northwest Airlines was threatened by a hostile takeover by a rich industrialist from out West. Concurrently, the Twin Cities of Minneapolis and St. Paul report a very healthy economy and a low unemployment rate. During the same time period, the University of Minnesota has not had a single takeover threat, nor has any other Minnesota public sector organization experienced one, though the donation-supported and nonprofit Minnesota Ballet recently went out of business. A year from now I am sure there will be similar reports about other Minnesota organizations, with the great bulk of the news being from the private sector.

Business decision makers—typically, people with titles of manager, director, vice-president, president, or CEO—are charged with making all kinds of decisions that contribute to the fundamental economic missions of their firms. They evaluate continually and make decisions based on their evaluations. Rarely do they evaluate and act in a manner comparable with the theories and practices of program evaluators, who have a public sector orientation. Evaluation experts usually focus on examining effects of programs (Phillips, 1983; Parker, 1986). Corporate decision makers focus on making up-front choices (Swanson and Gradous, 1988). One simple way of viewing these differences is to think of the decision maker as a venture capitalist who makes big business decisions on selected information. In contrast, the professional evaluator is viewed as an accountant who tediously adds up the pennies already spent. The bold venture capitalist relies on quick timing and choosing the best option, while the cautious accountant waits for all the data before filing an accurate report.

The discrepancy between the needs of the decision makers in business and the solutions espoused by many evaluation theorists is so great that I regularly ask the provoking question, "Will program evaluation scholars like this?" If the answer is no, I then consider that I might be on the right track.

The Nature of the Private Sector

A number of conceptual models describe the business context in which private sector training operates. The Tichy, Frombrun, and Devanna (1982) model is comfortable for both business people and scholars. The elements of the firm, according to this model, include mission and strategy, organizational structure, and human resources management. The societal forces include political, economic, and cultural factors.

For an analogy, we can use the conceptual model of the firm as the subject matter and the evaluator as a photographer. The photographer chooses among cameras; some have lenses that can zoom in or out. This lens movement, plus other intricacies of a camera and its operation, metaphorically represent the evaluator's expertise and toolbox. To the typical evaluation expert, the end produced—the picture—is the evaluation report. To the industrialist, the evaluation report is only one means to some other end within the business milieu of the firm. Many other things are going on in the firm, typically more than can be reasonably comprehended. Thus, the private sector decision maker agonizes about the options, their potential contribution to the business mission and strategy, and the relative cost and benefits of each option.

In my personal life I most often choose the simplest solution that will yield me the quality standard I desire. To return to the camera metaphor, my personal camera is a $79.95 model. The relative costs (financial and operational) and benefits (picture quality) of my daughter's $300 camera do not even interest me. I could take up two pages explaining why the $79.95 camera is perfect for me. However, most photography experts tend to snub my $79.95 solution. When they criticize, I simply cut those camera experts out of my photography decision-making process. Similarly, program evaluation experts are regularly cut out of the private sector training activity. Occasionally, at the training department's equivalent of the photographer's "weddings and proms," the experts are invited in to provide evaluation services. For example, the new human resources director, who manages all the human resources functions and who has no expertise in training, may hire an outside consultant to evaluate the training department. Another example would be the training manager who hires an external evaluator to assess the effectiveness of a company-wide, participative management training effort.

It is important to note, so as to round out the scenario, that evaluation experts are also critical of the typical training-evaluation practices in the private sector and what they generally see as training-evaluation practices that contain major threats to validity (Campbell, 1971; Parker, 1986).

Efficiency and Effectiveness

The general business decision framework embraces the values of effectiveness and efficiency. Most public sector decision makers use the rhetoric of effectiveness and are constrained by controlled costs. Managers in the public sector are generally more verbal than their private sector counterparts. The public sector managers "talk" their way into success, and private sector managers "perform" their way into success. Thus, the public sector rhetoric often gets way out of line with the available resources. Since public sector rhetoric and accountability are with different constituencies, the loop is rarely closed as it is in the private sector.

In an elementary way, efficiency can be thought of as the cost side of the formula, and effectiveness the benefit side. In the private sector, however, return-on-investment (ROI) reigns supreme. Within firms, some business units are directly connected to benefits (or income generation), and others are considered overhead costs (or burden). For the training department positioned as overhead, cost control is paramount. A good training manager in this context reduces the training budget. When training is positioned as a business partner, that is, as a person expected to directly increase profits, performance improvement related to the goods and services provided by the firm is critical. A good training manager in this context increases units of work performance that have value to the firm. A very obvious example is with a firm that sells training as a product and service. A U.S. producer of portable data collectors used for statistical process control of manufactured goods also sells data collector training and statistical process control training to its hardware customers. The training manager reports to the national sales director and is evaluated on his or her dollar sales of training. Additionally, the training manager has financial incentives in the form of a commission beyond the base salary.

Most firms are not in the business of training employees or customers except when doing so contributes directly to the total performance of the organization. It is costly to train people. If possible, training, as with any other high-cost activity that is not making an important performance contribution, will be eliminated from the corporate budget. Decision makers generally decide to support training as a business decision with the purpose of improving performance, maintaining performance, or fulfilling compliance requirements.

In some instances training is forced on an organization by law or by regulatory agencies. For example, many chemical, manufacturing, and service industries are required by law to train employees in handling chemicals in order to protect their workers and the general public. Likewise, a small custodial firm can be held legally accountable for informing its employees about and protecting them from the cleaning agents they use in their work. The controversy surrounding the asbestos industry has been well publicized and has gained great public attention. Lives have been lost as a result of exposure to asbestos and asbestos-producing firms have been economically crippled or put out of business as a result of litigation.

Compliance training is a serious matter, and the role of evaluation is to document that the training did, in fact, take place. Even so, documentation such as content outlines, samples of handout materials, and attendance records will likely exceed the evaluation required for compliance training. Such crude evaluations as attendance at safety training, when viewed through the photographer metaphor, are analogous to a child's use of a cheap plastic camera containing film that develops before her eyes—instant documentation. The photographs may be fuzzy and poorly framed, but they are good enough for the situation.

Foundations of Training

A number of years ago I presented the notion that there are two foundational bodies of knowledge for training: psychology and economics (Swanson, 1982, 1987). In a more recent discussion of the role of training and organizational performance, Campbell (1988) acknowledges this perspective. The psychological (educational) foundation of training is primarily focused on the development and implementation of training. The economic (managerial) foundation focuses on the organizational needs assessment and the ultimate contribution of training to organizational performance.

When performed correctly, systematic training in industry and business does not start with the assumption that there is a need for training. Many scholars of education, as well as those who articulate the dominant public sector view, assume that education or training is needed. In contrast, private sector training begins by questioning the need for improved organization or individual performance, then further questions the probability that reality training will influence that performance. Training systems, such as the Training Technology System (see Figure A.1), carefully connect the training function to performance at both ends of the system (Swanson, 1987).

The learning, human development perspective is the view held by the majority of the practitioners in the training profession. Concurrently, the economic performance, or human capital view, is the perspective held by the majority of the private sector decision makers, who most likely were not trained to be trainers.

Private sector training-evaluation efforts are framed by the two foundational areas of economics and psychology and by the quest for efficiency and effectiveness. These four elements provide a useful matrix for examining training evaluation (see Figure A.2).

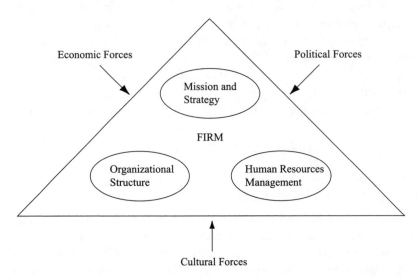

FIGURE A.1   Model of the Firm (Tichy, Frombrun, and Devanna 1982)

Most program evaluation experts focus on the psychological row of the matrix in terms of behaviors or processes of changing behaviors. This psychological focus, by itself, can be fundamentally out of line with the private sector economic agenda.

The psychology-efficiency cell focuses on speeding up the learning process or on utilizing fewer resources in a set time period through the application of sound learning theory and educational technology. Another way of increasing efficiency is to reduce the inefficiencies of and barriers to learning that typically exist in unstructured training, such as self-managed, trial-and-error-learning.

Evaluation at the efficiency level is process-oriented and formative in nature. Such evaluations are used to improve the training/learning process. The substance of process control and improvement evaluation activity is important for professional trainers but is of little interest to nontrainers and others whose perspective primarily represents the economic/business concerns of organizations.

The economic-efficiency cell focuses on reducing or containing costs. Almost all businesses have fairly elaborate cost-accounting systems and methods. Furthermore, most work groups are financially monitored by someone in their respective firms. Categories of costs include fixed, variable, direct,

Table A.2　Training-Evaluation Framework

Productivity	Foundations of Training	
	Economics	*Psychology*
Efficiency	Reduce or maintain dollar/performance cost	Reduce or maintain trainee anxiety
Effectiveness	Maintain or increase dollar/performance benefit	Maintain or increase trainee expertise

charge-back/overhead and marginal/step costs (Head, 1985; Swanson and Gradous, 1988). Training departments and other departments seen as overhead are closely monitored through management information systems for the purpose of controlling costs or spotting cost-cutting opportunities. Even while this monitoring is going on, it is not common for this cost information to be fully shared with the training department or the personnel being evaluated. Furthermore, it is very possible for management to establish a training cost-reduction or cost containment goal without directly communicating this to the training manager. At the present time there are many corporate takeovers in process in American business. Many of these firms, in an attempt to retain existing ownership status, will systematically cut staff and functions for the purpose of lowering costs and increasing profits. Units not directly connected to the economic-efficiency cell are candidates for such cuts. Human resource departments in these firms that are grounded in the "psychology only" perspective are invariably cut.

The competent training manager, working in a cost-reduction or cost-containment environment, can increase training quantity and quality by entertaining new alternatives. Evaluation should help plan and verify these efforts. Creative managers can look at high-cost items such as especially costly programs or costly phases of programs and begin brainstorming options, evaluating these options to see if they deliver comparable results. Since training-development and delivery costs can be very high, the use of an "off-the-shelf" program may save on development costs. Self-instruction also may save on delivery costs. The development of new partnerships with the stakeholders in the training context, thus sharing responsibility for training, may also reduce costs. The point is, given the many training options available, there are possibilities for providing the same performance results at reduced costs. This kind of thinking is private sector thinking and the kind that evaluators should help trainers to pursue.

For example, the service training department of a manufacturing organization faced such a cost-containment condition. The department had been providing "free training" to independent distributors. In response to their cost-containment goal, they produced programmed instruction and trained their distributors to manage the training. They realized an $80,000 cost reduction, which they reinvested in other opportunities.

Learning and Satisfaction

The psychology-effectiveness cell in Figure A.2 is familiar to most evaluation experts (Brinkerhoff, 1987); the associated techniques being well developed and widely used. Here the focus is on trainee satisfaction and learning. The traditional, private sector training-evaluation practice of measuring participant satisfaction and the public sector practice of measuring participant learning are well understood by both professional trainers and evaluation experts. Trainers are often seen by evaluation experts as giving too much credence to measures of trainee satisfaction, while trainers generally believe that evaluation experts overemphasize formal measures of learning (Sleezer, 1989). As an additional difference, I have also observed that most private sector trainers live in a culture of "customer satisfaction," whereas most public sector educational evaluators live in a culture of "gains in knowledge."

Trainers generally focus learning measures on the very specific work behaviors that they are expected to develop in employees. They thus provide in-training exercises to satisfy trainees and others that learning has taken place. Some examples of specific work behaviors are the following: (1) Managers need to know the purpose of the XYZ Corporation employee-appraisal system and the method of completing the forms. (2) Aluminum extruder operators need to know how to start up, operate, troubleshoot, and shut down the "ACME Extruder."

To ensure effective work behaviors in these and other specific domains, trainers emphasize up-front analysis of work behavior to make sure the content is right (Swanson and Gradous, 1986; Carlisle, 1986). They then construct tests to check whether this content has been learned. In-training performance and performance tests (to a lesser extent) are valued over after-the-fact tests of knowledge.

Attempts to simplify the measures of satisfaction and to expand the measures of satisfaction beyond the trainees to the trainee's supervisors are frequent among private sector trainers (Swanson and Sleezer, 1987). For example, lengthy satisfaction questionnaires, often seen in public sector education programs, are reduced to the core purpose of training and core values of the organization. Core questions for participants typically include the following: Was the training delivered professionally? Were the learning objectives met? Was the original need met? Was the training valuable? Core questions for the participant's supervisor would only include the last two items. This is because supervisors did not directly experience the training.

Clearly, there are multiple "customers" of training in the business context and they should be taken seriously by trainers. Supervisors that allow their employees to go to training pay a price. That price is sometimes a direct budget transfer and almost always includes time away from regular work (which still needs to be completed). To ignore this decision maker in the training process would be very shortsighted.

Economic Effects

The economic-effectiveness cell in Figure A.2 is the bugaboo of the training profession and has not been well developed by evaluators. The evaluation options in this cell range from the accountant's perspective (Flamholtz, 1985) to the venture capitalist's perspective (Swanson and Gradous, 1988). Each financial perspective provides a powerful view of the position of training in the organization. To a top manager, not being able to talk about training from a financial perspective is almost worse than having inaccurate numbers. The private sector culture is a financial numbers culture. If trainers cannot even attempt to talk about their corporate activities in terms of financial indices, they are almost automatically placed off to the side or "out of the ballpark." If they can talk financial numbers, right or wrong, they are at least "in the ballpark." Once there, they and others can refine the measures.

Top managers in business and industry view and value training through an economic lens. These nontraining decision makers will mentally fill in the financial picture on training with or without the actual financial data. The risk is that, in most instances, this off-the-cuff analysis is inaccurate and not supportive of training.

As the cost and demand for training have increased, the demand for financial data on training is coming from top management, not from training professionals. But there are some promising new trends. One important method that some training professionals are using to move into the "economic-effectiveness" cell is the use of a training-for-performance orientation. Through critical investments in up-front training needs analyses, trainers identify important performance opportunities and needs that training can solve (Rossett, 1987). Subsequent back-on-the-job increases in performance provide excellent proxies for economic effectiveness in business and industry. Once the training opportunities and needs are isolated and pursued, the evaluator obtains actual measures of performance in the workplace. So it was with a very large health maintenance organization. After struggling with how to measure the effectiveness of a company-wide organizational development effort to "be nice to the customer," they finally came down to the numbers of subscribers as the performance measure. That is, the "nice/not nice" impression eventually translated to customer subscriptions. In this instance, the human resources development program and the measure of effectiveness were at the heart of the organization.

The key to the economic-effectiveness perspective is to get trainers to focus on "performance needs" and to get corporate decision makers to "want" what they need. A "wants" analysis will surely yield very specific requests for training programs, and going around asking people what they want is easy and comfortable. But very often those wants have nothing to do with the performance needs or problems that organizations and individual employees face because careful performance analysis is not required by the "wants" assessment. For example, managers in a large manufacturing firm said that they wanted cross-training for all their production employees to help cover work during absences and vacations. At the very same time, an incredible 48 percent of their product was turning out as scrap. For any number of reasons, the employees did not even know their own jobs, let alone their neighbor's jobs. The need for operator training was great. The need for operator cross-training was minimal given the urgent quality control problem.

Most important aspects of businesses already have been evaluated. Examples include units produced, cost per unit, accident-free days, sales per salesperson or sales region, number of customers, scrap rates, customer satisfaction, dollar sales, and a variety of other quality indices. Since most important aspects of firms are evaluated, the training evaluator may only need to look at ongoing organizational or employee-performance measures before and after training to get at the appropriate economic effectiveness measures. Of course, evaluators still must work before and after training to link training results to these important aspects of business.

Summary

An understanding of the language of the private sector is critical to evaluators. The evaluation expert who plans to work in the private sector should refer back to the opening sentence of this chapter: "The mission and goal of business and industry are to maximize the economic return on investment through the production and sale of goods and services." Clearly, the values and vocabulary of business differ greatly from the values and vocabulary of traditional public sector evaluation.

One simple, but important, means to understanding the full and realistic potential of training evaluation is to study the values and the vocabulary of business and industry. I believe that such an effort will change the evaluation expert's view of evaluation and increase the expert's potential for improving training in industry and business. Two concrete personal examples include the business and industry concepts of auditing and process improvement.

I worked with Brian Murphy, a business person, on the concept of auditing training (Murphy and Swanson, 1988). This was a very direct effort at taking the business language and methods of financial auditing and using them to develop a process for auditing the training function in the private sector. We sampled each step of the training process to see whether there were departures from sound practices. Only where such departures were identified was further evaluation (a costly process) pursued. New priorities, not just new words, appeared. Furthermore, the information generated from this auditing process did not exceed the requirements of the decisions to be made.

A second example is when I worked with Catherine Sleezer in the area of training-process improvement and control (Sleezer and Swanson, 1989). We were working with an electronics manufacturing firm that has a complex manufacturing system in need of a great deal of process control to keep it running (and to improve it). Conceptually, we identified a similar need for a training-process control system for the training department, and important new evaluation ideas emerged for us. In both of these examples, the values and language of the businesses involved greatly influenced the training-evaluation language and methods we proposed.

A second simple, but important, means of understanding the full and realistic potential of training evaluation is to study the existing measures of performance in any one business or industry. The title of this chapter contains the clue: "Everything important in business and industry is evaluated."

While this statement is most likely an exaggeration, I have witnessed too many evaluation experts running around trying to invent measures that are compatible with their own values. Evaluation experts should cull the performance measures already used in and valued by firms. Training that is not connected to these measures should be questioned, and evaluation of training should incorporate these measures.

Evaluation of the effectiveness of an ongoing training program in terms of existing measures of organizational and individual performance is a powerful means of getting a firm to think critically about the purpose of training (Swanson and Sleezer, 1987). In the process, decision makers often ask, "Why did we approve this program?" At that point, the training and nontraining personnel are usually ready to think about training as a means to some large business goal, and evaluation as a way of helping to make wise decisions along the way.

Appendix B:
Demonstrating the
Financial Benefit of
Human Resource Development

Status and Update on the Theory and Practice

Richard A. Swanson
University of Minnesota

A serious problem facing the HRD profession is the perception from managers that HRD is not a good investment. Furthermore, a recent study of HRD practices reports that only 3 percent of the programs in HRD are evaluated in terms of financial impact. Yet, the research clearly demonstrates that HRD interventions focused on performance improvement deliver 8:1 return-on-investment in a year or less. This appendix reports this financial benefit research and proposes new areas of financial research.

A recent business page headline from London's *Daily Telegraph* reads "Training falls down on the job."(October 27, 1997, p. 31). This report was based on a study of business leaders. The popular perception that HRD costs organizations more than it returns in benefits has haunted the human resource development (HRD) profession since its inception. And, not being

Reprinted with permission: *Human Resource Development Quarterly 9* (3) (1998) 285-295.

able to change this perception is the Achilles' heel of HRD. While organizations are more than economic entities— organizations are economic entities. Any organization that remains alive will ultimately judge each of its components from a return-on-investment (ROI) framework and they will do it with or without valid data.

To face this challenge, four views of HRD have been presented to the HRD profession. They are: (1) a major business process, something an organization must do to succeed, (2) a value-added activity, something that is potentially worth doing, (3) an optional activity, something that is nice to do, and (4) a waste of business resources, something that has costs exceeding the benefits (Swanson, 1995).

The dominant view of HRD is within options 3 and 4 above— HRD as being an optional activity or having costs greater than its benefits. The simple idea that HRD is not a good investment is popular and entrenched. Economist Paul Krugman (1994) informs us of the dangers of pop economics and the fact that simple ideas [right or wrong] have staying power.

A recent study by the ASTD, the profession's largest practitioner organization, reports that in terms of actual evaluation of HRD programs in the field, "three percent are evaluated for financial impact." (Bassi, Benson, & Cheney, 1996, p. 11). The irony is that ASTD has been the chief advocate of the profession's most widely endorsed evaluation scheme, Donald Kirkpatrick's simple, yet flawed and impotent, four-level evaluation model (Alliger & Janak, 1989; Holton, 1996). Even Kirkpatrick's recent best selling book is void of any elementary economic or psychometric theory (see Kirkpatrick, 1994).

Problem Statement, Historical Framework, and Research Questions

Decision makers in organizations must work up budgets, justify their own salaries, and propose strategies, projects, and programs to top management. Unlike other managers, HRD people tend to resist doing these tasks. The most likely reasons for this are that they originally chose their profession because they were hands-on and people oriented and not inclined toward the financial side of the organization.

A Short History.   Economic thinking related to human capacity, human expertise, and human effort and the effects of each is disjointed. History provides a fairly consistent notion that there is much to be gained by being purposeful in managing these domains. Throughout history, the ideological responses to capturing the spoils of human expertise have ranged from communes, to slavery, to meritocracies. Whatever the ideology— "There's money in those skills!"

The importance of increasing one's expertise is confirmed in society's comparisons of educational levels and economic success. Even so, investments in the development of its personnel is still not a clear option for most firms. Organizations can access expertise in ways other than offering development programs. For example, they can hire expertise and/or establish the expectation that employees will manage the development of their own expertise. Neither of these two options require an organization to make direct financial outlays for HRD.

For the HRD profession, the "Training Within Industry" project (Dooley, 1945) was a watershed. This 1940–45 massive national performance improvement effort clearly and consistently demonstrated the economic impact of HRD and the required conditions for achieving financial benefits.

In the 1960s and 1970s a renaissance in the profession provided incentive to think more about HRD as an investment. The literature increasingly reported financial analysis methods (FAM) and studies of programs' costs and benefits (Cullen, Sawzin, Sisson, & Swanson, 1976, 1978; Gilbert, 1978; Meissner, 1964; Swanson & Sawzin, 1975). In the 1980s this financial analysis trend continued with a greater focus on costs and the human resource management perspective versus performance improvement (Cascio, 1987; Flamholtz, 1985; Head, 1985; Kearsley, 1982; Spencer, 1986). These company-wide FAMs took an accounting perspective rather than a performance improvement perspective.

To the 1980s, FAM efforts in HRD did not address the decision-making dilemmas faced by organizations at the investment decision stage of their organizational planning. Difficult as it may seem, any organization can conduct an after-the-fact cost-benefit analysis . What was needed was a method for forecasting those costs and benefits, at the point of making investment decisions. The forecasting financial benefits (FFB) of HRD method was designed to fill this gap (Swanson, Lewis, & Boyer, 1982; Swanson & Geroy, 1983; Swanson & Gradous, 1988). The FFB is a practical step-by-step method for making accurate investment decisions based on forecasting (1) the financial value of improved performance projections for a program, (2) the cost of implementing a program, and (3) the return on the program investment (Swanson & Gradous, 1988). The FFB method is best suited to short term HRD interventions purposefully connected to performance deficiencies. The problem facing the FFB method is that it is not as easily applied to large scale change, long-term change, and to interventions loosely connected to performance requirements.

Research Questions. The following three questions serve as the basis of this inquiry:

1. What core findings relevant to the financial analysis of HRD have appeared in the literature?
2. What core findings relevant to the forecasting of financial benefits of HRD have appeared in the literature?
3. What new FAM theories and tools have been reported in the literature that HRD should pursue?

Core Financial Analysis Method (FAM)

The core FAM method, based upon several years of research, has proven to be a helpful tool to overcome the difficult and often resisted problem of talking about human resource development in dollar and cents terms (Swanson & Gradous, 1988). The model and method for analyzing actual and forecasted financial benefits are relatively simple and straightforward. They both have three main components: (1) the performance value resulting from the program, (2) the cost of the program, and (3) the benefit resulting from the program.

The basic financial analysis model is:

Performance Value

— Cost

Benefit

The FAM method is an expansion of the three components into three separate worksheets. Readers wishing to receive detailed instruction on the should obtain the author's full text (Swanson & Gradous, 1988). For a broad overview of FAMs in context of HRD, see Mosier (1990). In addition, the bibliography serves to capture important literature related to the financial analysis of HRD beyond just those studies cited directly in this paper.

Five Early HRD Financial Analysis Classics. There is a substantial cache of HRD economic research. Unfortunately, it spread throughout the refereed, non-refereed, HRD, and non-HRD literature and generally is not in the hands of HRD decision makers. Five early classics provide excellent examples. In chronological order, each is briefly abstracted:

1. *The training within industry report, 1910–1945. Washington, DC: War Manpower Commission Bureau of Training, Training Within Industry Service.*

While this 330 page report of a massive five-year nation-wide effort is not a research report, it contains data sprinkled throughout on the financial results of sample TWI programs that are worth noting. The refrain of TWI personnel was, "Will it fix a production problem?" If not, they did not support the program. When they did support a program, they were able to track the results. The optical lens grinding case study established a $15 value to the quality completion of a grinding task (p. 271–292). At the time, this financial value was quite significant and was magnified by the large number of new workers needed to grind lenses. In another report, improved methods at one arsenal were determined to exceed a savings of $1,000,000.

2. *Meissner, F. (1964). Measuring quantitatively the effect of personnel training. Training Directors Journal. 18(3), 230–236.*

This study of "simple" work behavior, bagging groceries, compared bagging training to no-training. The underlying premise was that there is a right or optimal way of doing any work and that there are financial consequences to expertise. A major paper manufacturer conducted 20 in-store experiments to determine the cost-effectiveness of a training program in "bagsmanship." The dependent variable was bag costs. The study concluded that there is an 8:1 ROI on the training investment if stores paid for the training materials and 11:1 ROI for stores if the bag supplier paid for the training materials portion of the cost. The further assumption was that the consideration of damaged goods and improved customer relations would increase the ROI.

3. *Thomas, B., Moxham, J., & Jones, J.G.G. (1969). A cost benefit analysis of industrial training. British Journal of Industrial Relations, 7(2), 231–264.*

This study compared the cost-effectiveness of two alternative forms of general training for clothing machine operators (labeled "new" and "old"). The analysis was based on a comparison of performance among 139 old and 92 new trainee/workers over a four year period. The dependent variables were performance levels, retention, and length of the training period. It was found that the average performance level of new trainee/workers increased as much as 30% during the first year following innovative training and then leveled off. The ratio of benefits to costs over the four year period was 8:1.

4. Swanson, R. A., & Sawzin, S. A. (1975). Industrial training research project. Bowling Green, OH: Bowling Green State University. (also reported later in the literature as: Cullen, G., Sawzin, S., Sisson, G. R., & Swanson, R. A. (1976). Training, what's it worth? Training and Development Journal, 30(8), 12–20).

This controlled experimental study compared structured on-the-job training to unstructured on-the-job training for two groups of 20 semi-skilled extrusion molder operators. The dependent variable was expertise in being able to produce "quality plastic pipe." The results of this study concluded that the training time required to reach competence under unstructured training was significantly higher (p<.005) than the structured method (16.3 versus 4.55 hours), structured training workers produced significantly less waste (p<.01) and solved significantly more production problems (p<.025), and that the financial break-even point in absorbing the development and delivery costs of structured training for trainees (compared to no development and delivery costs of unstructured on-the-job training) was at 10 trainees. Every trainee beyond the 10 represents additional ROI on the existing training investment. Extension of the data to the actual numbers of employees requiring training yielded a 10:1 ROI in a two month period.

5. Rosentreter, G. E. (1979). Economic evaluation of a training program. In R. O. Peterson (Ed.) Studies in Training and Development: Research Papers from the 1978 ASTD National Conference. Madison, WI: ASTD Press.

This financial analysis of an adult education program offered through a community college to company managers focused on communication skills for goal setting. Of the 68 managers, 34 attended the 15 hour communication skills training. The dependent variables were employee turnover, employee punctuality, and grievances. The results in all three domains were compared between the employees reporting to the trained and untrained supervisors. There was no significant difference in the punctuality and numbers of grievances filed between the experimental and control groups. There was a significant difference in turnover that turnover was financially analyzed. Given the financial consequences of the reduced turnover, there was a 9:1 ROI for the communication skills training.

Summary.   The research results from these varied studies were quite consistent. They demonstrated that HRD imbedded in a purposeful performance improvement framework yielded very high returns on investments, an ROI of 8:1 or more in a year or less.

From Financial Analysis of Methods (FAM) to Forecasting Financial Benefits (FFB)

There are a substantial number of studies in the realm of forecasting the financial benefits of HRD. This FFB literature is also dispersed in the HRD literature. Again, five studies have been identified, presented in chronological order, and briefly abstracted.

1. Geroy, G. D., & Swanson, R. A. (1984). Forecasting training costs and benefits in industry. Journal of Epsilon Pi Tau, 10(2), 15–19.

This study forecasted the financial benefits of a geometric dimension and tolerancing training program for 136 Onan Corporation employees. Using the FFB method, mangers forecasted ROIs of 7:1, 11:1, 11:1, and 22:1. All agreed that the training would be a sound investment for the corporation. The follow-up financial analysis of actual performance of two trained workers yielded a ROI of 27:1 on one and 159:1 on another. This ideal situation had relevant, low-cost training ($80.50 per employee) and high gain application opportunities in the workplace. In this study, the benefits derived from just two employees paid for training all 136 employees and then some.

2. Swanson, R. A. & Gradous, D. B. (1988). Forecasting financial benefits of human resource development. San Francisco: Jossey-Bass.

This comprehensive book puts forth the theory and practice of forecasting the financial benefits (FFB) of human resource development. Also included in the book are eight cases and supporting data from actual organizations. The ROI of all these cases met or exceeded 8:1.

3. Swanson, R. A. & Sleezer, C. M. (1989). Determining financial benefits of an organization development program. Performance Improvement Quarterly, 2(1) 55–65.

This study from a health maintenance organization reports the forecasted and actual performance values, costs, and benefits from a complex company-wide organization development intervention that was combined with an aggressive marketing campaign. The dependent variable was "members." The forecasting portion of the study yielded underestimates of the actual data, but led to valid investment decisions, the purpose of the forecasting method. Thus, this phase further validated the FFB method. In terms of the total actual performance value resulting from the performance improvement effort, two top executives were called upon to estimate the relative contribution of the marketing and organization development components to the total 12.5 million dollar gain. One executive estimated the OD performance value contribution resulting from the $44,590 OD investment as $5,040,000 (11:1 ROI) and the other estimated it to be $7,452,000 (16.4:1 ROI).

4. Jacobs, R., Jones, M., & Neil, S. (1992). A case study in forecasting the financial benefits of unstructured and structured on-the-job training. Human Resource Development Quarterly, 3(2), 133–139.

This case study compared the forecasted financial benefits between unstructured and structured forms of on-the-job training. The setting of a large truck-assembly plant and a focus on three production job tasks resulted in the forecasted structured OJT performance value being twice the performance value of unstructured OJT at the end of an equivalent evaluation period. From a ROI perspective, the forecasted $39.04 average training cost per worker on task #1 resulted in an added average performance gain of $16,065 over the unstructured training option. This resulted in a forecasted 411:1 ROI for the training investment. The forecasted $195.20 average training cost per worker on task #2 resulted in an added average performance gain of $3,174.75 over the unstructured training option. This resulted in a forecasted 16:1 ROI for the training investment. The forecasted $139.40 average training cost per worker on task #3 resulted in a added average performance gain of $8,889.30 over the unstructured training option. This resulted in a forecasted 63:1 ROI for the training investment.

5. Clements, J. C. & Josiam, B. M. (1995). Training: quantifying the financial benefits. International Journal of Contemporary Hospitality Management, 7(1), 10–15.

This case study applied the FFB method to an actual small hotel franchise disguised as BUDSYS Hotels (they have traditionally relied on the buddy system of training new employees). The dependent variable was front desk transactions. The case goes on to forecast the performance values, training costs, and benefits of unstructured buddy-system training to a structured self-tutorial package. The forecasted $81,000 performance gain from the structured training over the unstructured option represents a forecasted 8.7:1 ROI in three months.

Summary   These studies clearly demonstrate that HRD can be a very sound financial investment. The research further provides evidence that HRD interventions focused on appropriate dependent performance variables and systematically executed will financially forecast and return 8:1 or more. In contrast, there is no evidence that unfocused and unsystematic

HRD interventions yield positive returns or returns that even exceed their costs.

Update from Recent Financial Analysis Research

There is a substantial array of new HRD related economic research studies. In chronological order, five selected studies are briefly abstracted along with implications for HRD.

1. D'Aveni, R. A. & Ravensscraft, D. J. (1994). Economies of integration versus bureaucracy costs: Does vertical integration improve performance? Academy of Management Journal. 37(5), 1167–1206.

D'Aveni and Ravensscraft (1994) studied vertical integration, cost structure, and performance at the line-of-business level. They concluded that vertical integration results in overall lowered costs in spite of the additional bureaucratic costs. Vertical integration cost reductions "may arise from transaction-related costs, shared common costs, and enhanced productivity" (p. 1193). The effect on HRD when an organization alters its structure (e.g. vertical integration) is fundamental and the ability of HRD to be central to the organization is dependent on its ability (1) to respond systemically (bureaucratically) and (2) to demonstrate its economic contributions (improvements in transaction-related costs, shared common costs, and enhanced productivity). The structural impact on HRD has to do with alignment with business unit versus having a function and programs that transcend sub-units. While opinions sway over time, the economics of these organization strategies for HRD should be studied.

2. Romanelli, E. & Tushman, M. L. (1994). Organizational transformation as punctuated equilibrium: An empirical test. Academy of Management Journal, 37(5) 1141–1166.

Romanelli and Tushman report that "small change in strategies, structures, and power distributions did not accumulate to produce fundamental transformations" (p. 1141). Their view of revolutionary change largely discounts HRD transformational theories and practices of working from the bottom-up or from the middle-out. They further conclude that the popular cascading model of change within a framework of interdependent relationships actually resists change and prevents small changes in organizational sub-units from taking hold. This and other similar studies challenges the viability of HRD to be a major contributor to the long-term economic vitality of an organization and deserve further research. The results of this line of research would ultimately challenge and refine the mission of HRD and how it positions itself in the organization.

3. Hendricks, K. B. & Singhal, V. R. (1995). Does implementing an effective TQM program actually improve operating performance? Empirical evidence from firms that have won quality awards. Williamsburg, VA: School of Business, College of William and Mary.

This study, sponsored by the US Labor Department, pursues the hypothesizes as to the effectiveness of TQM on firm performance. TQM companies showed significant gains in the dependent variables of operating income and sales growth, capital expenditures, employment growth, and total assets compared to the sample of control group of firms. There were no significant differences in cost control. This study of company-wide implementation of an intensive personnel development intervention (TQM) and the utilization of standard economic performance data over time as compared to a control group of firms casts a large economic analysis net. Comparisons of the economic performance of multiple firms that invest in their human resources compared to those that do not need to be studied by the profession. Such studies would serve to better understand the economic contribution of the human capital to an organization.

4. Lyau, N. M., Pucel, D. J. (1995). Economic return on training at the organization level. Performance Improvement Quarterly, 8(3), 68–79.

This study examined labor-productivity returns from investments in a manufacturing industry and its 237 large and medium-sized firms. Two labor-productivity dependent variables (sales per worker and direct costs of training) and two training investment dependent variables (total training costs and direct costs of training) were studied. A significant relationship between investments in training and labor productivity as measured by value added per worker was found. This is defined as the dollar value of products sold, minus the cost of the materials in those products, divided by the number of workers. On the average, firms increasing their training expenditure by 10% could expect a 1.0% to 1.2% increase in the level of labor productivity. Studies that lead to core generalizations as to the return on company-wide expenditures are needed to advance HRD's status in the operational budgeting process.

5. Swanson, R. A. & Mattson, B. W. (1997). Development and validation of the critical outcome technique (COT). In R. Torraco (Ed.) Academy of Human Resource Development 1996 Annual Proceedings. 64–71.

The COT represents a unique development in post-hoc program evaluation. Until now, the primary avenue of being able to predictably demonstrate the financial results of HRD has been through a systematic development process including up-front performance analysis and systematic evaluation. The COT is conceptually similar to the famed Critical Incident Technique in that it functions within the milieu of an ongoing organization while yielding critical outcome data. The five steps include (1) outcome verification, (2) outcome inquiry, (3) outcome verification and attribution, (4) outcome valuation, and (5) outcome report (see Swanson, 1996; Mattson, Quartanna, & Swanson, 1998). Metaphorically, the COT is a "strategy for finding the needle [financial performance] in the haystack [organization]" and could be an appropriate and powerful tool for validating the financial impact of certain HRD interventions.

Summary.　Each of these studies provide a challenge and opportunity in the financial analysis of HRD benefits. Furthermore, each is worthy of further research.

Conclusion

Economics has been purported to be one of the foundational theories of the HRD discipline. As such, it is critical to continually update the status of the economic theories and practices relevant to HRD. While the existing FAM methods available to the HRD profession are too rarely used, updating the theory and methodology may serve to change this condition.

Appendix C:

Reproducible Forms for Assessing Financial Benefits of Human Resource Development

Program _____ Analyst _____ Date _____

Time-Performance Graph

Program/Intervention _____ Analyst _____ Date _____

	Option name: 1_____	2_____
Data required for calculations:		
(a) What unit of performance are you measuring?	_____ unit name	_____ unit name
(b) What is the performance goal per worker/group/system at the end of your HRD program?	___ ____ / ___ no. units / time	___ ____ / ___ no. units / time
(c) What is the performance per worker/group/system at the beginning of the HRD program?	___ ____ / ___ no. units / time	___ ____ / ___ no. units / time
(d) What dollar value is assigned to each performance unit?	$_____/unit	$_____/unit
(e) What is the development time required to reach the expected performance level?	_____ _____ no. time	_____ _____ no. time
(f) What is the assessment period? (Enter the longest time (e) of all options being considered.)	_____ _____ no. time	_____ _____ no. time
(g) How many workers/groups/systems will participate in your HRD program?	_____ no. workers/groups/ systems	_____ no. workers/groups/ systems
Calculations to determine net performance value:		
(h) Useable units workers/groups/systems produce during the HRD program? If no, enter -0-. If yes, enter known performance rate or calculate average performance rate [$(b + c)/2$]	_____ _____ no. units	_____ _____ no. units
(i) What are the total units per worker/group /system produced during the development time? (h x e)	_____ no. of units	_____ no. of units
(j) How many units produced per worker/work group/system during the assessment period? $\{[(f - e) \times b] + i\}$	_____ no. of units	_____ no. of units
(k) What is the value of the worker's/group's/system's performance during the assessment period? (j x d)	$ _____	$ _____
(l) What is the performance value gain per worker/group/system? [$k - (c \times d \times f)$]	$ _____	$ _____
(m) What is the total performance value gain for all workers/groups/systems? (l x g)	$ _____ (Option 1)	$ _____ (Option 2)

Note that performance units and time units for all options <u>must remain consistent</u> throughout the assessment.

Performance Value Worksheet

Program/Intervention _____ Analyst _____ Date _____

	Option name	1 _____	2 _____
Analyze			
Step 1	_____	_____	_____
Step 2	_____	_____	_____
Step 3	_____	_____	_____
Step 4	_____	_____	_____
Propose			
Step 1	_____	_____	_____
Step 2	_____	_____	_____
Step 3	_____	_____	_____
Step 4	_____	_____	_____
Create			
Step 1	_____	_____	_____
Step 2	_____	_____	_____
Step 3	_____	_____	_____
Step 4	_____	_____	_____
Implement			
Step 1	_____	_____	_____
Step 2	_____	_____	_____
Step 3	_____	_____	_____
Step 4	_____	_____	_____
Assess			
Step 1	_____	_____	_____
Step 2	_____	_____	_____
Step 3	_____	_____	_____
Step 4	_____	_____	_____
<u>Total costs</u>		$_____	$_____
		(Option 1)	(Option 2)

Cost Worksheet: Human Resource Development

Program/Intervention _____ Analyst _____ Date _____

Option name	1 _____	2 _____
Analyze:		
Diagnose performance	_____	_____
Document expertise	_____	_____
Other _____	_____	_____
Other _____	_____	_____
Design:		
Design program	_____	_____
Design lessons	_____	_____
Other _____	_____	_____
Other _____	_____	_____
Develop:		
Develop materials	_____	_____
Pilot test program	_____	_____
Other _____	_____	_____
Other _____	_____	_____
Implement:		
Manage program	_____	_____
Deliver training	_____	_____
Other _____	_____	_____
Other _____	_____	_____
Evaluate:		
Assess results	_____	_____
Report results	_____	_____
Other _____	_____	_____
Other _____	_____	_____
Total costs _____	$ _____	$ _____
	(Option 1)	(Option 2)

Cost Worksheet: Personnel Training and Development

Program/Intervention _____ Analyst _____ Date _____

Option name	1 _____	2 _____
1. Analyze & Contract		
Analyze	_____	_____
Contract	_____	_____
Other _____	_____	_____
Other _____	_____	_____
2. Diagnose & Feedback		
Diagnose	_____	_____
Feedback	_____	_____
Other _____	_____	_____
Other _____	_____	_____
3. Plan Design & Develop		
Plan	_____	_____
Design	_____	_____
Develop	_____	_____
Other _____	_____	_____
Other _____	_____	_____
4. Implement		
Manage	_____	_____
Deliver	_____	_____
Other _____	_____	_____
Other _____	_____	_____
5. Evaluate & Institutionalize		
Assess results	_____	_____
Report results	_____	_____
Institutionalize _____	_____	_____
Other _____	_____	_____
Total costs _____	$ _____	$ _____
	(Option 1)	(Option 2)

Cost Worksheet:Organization Development

Date _____

Program/Intervention _____ Analyst _____

Option	1 _____	2 _____
Performance Value	$ _____	$ _____
Minus Cost	_____	_____
Benefit	$ _____	$ _____

NOTE: Circle your choice of option.

Benefit Worksheet

References

Addicott, P. "ROI Model Gives Training New Respected Cost Justification." *Training Director's Forum Newsletter* 7, no. 6 (1991): 4–5.

Alliger, G., and E. Janak. "Kirkpatrick's Levels of Training Criteria: Thirty Years Later." *Personnel Psychology* 42, no. 2 (1989): 331–342.

Alliger, G., S. I. Tannenbaum, W. Bennett Jr., H. Traver, and A. Shotland. "A Meta-Analysis of the Relations Among Training Criteria." *Personnel Psychology* 50 (1997): 341–358.

Arvey, R., S. Maxwell, and E. Salas. "The Relative Power of Training Evaluation Designs Under Different Cost Configurations." *Journal of Applied Psychology* 77, no. 2 (1992): 155–160.

Bassi, L., G. Benson, and S. Cheney. "The Top Ten Trends." In *Trends: Position Yourself for the Future*, 2–16. Alexandria, Va.: ASTD Press, 1996.

Bassi, L. J., A. L. Gallagher, and E. Schroer. *The ASTD Training, Data Book*. Alexandria, Va.: ASTD Press, 1996.

Becker, G. S. *Human Capital: A Theoretical and Empirical Analysis with Special Reference to Education, 3d ed.* Chicago: University of Chicago Press, 1993.

Blomberg, R. "Cost-Benefit Analysis of Employee Training: A Literature Review." *Adult Education Quarterly* 39, no. 2 (1989): 89–98.

Bohan, G., and N. Horney. "Pinpointing the Real Cost of Quality in a Service Company." *National Productivity Review* 10, no. 3 (1991): 309–317.

Boudreau, J. W., and P. M. Ramstad. *Measuring Intellectual Capital: Learning from Financial History*. Ithaca, N.Y.: Cornell University Center for Advanced Human Resource Studies.

Brethower, D. "Strategic Improvement of Workplace Competence II: The Economics of Competence." *Performance Improvement Quarterly* 6, no. 2 (1993): 29–42.

Brinkerhoff, R. O. *Achieving Results from Training: How to Evaluate Human Resource Development to Strengthen Programs and Increase Impact.* San Francisco: Jossey-Bass, 1987.

Brinkerhoff, R. O., ed. "Evaluating Training Programs in Business and Industry." *New Directions for Program Evaluation* 44. San Francisco: Jossey-Bass, winter 1989.

Campbell, J. "Personnel, Training, and Development." *Annual Review of Psychology* 22 (1971): 565–595.

––––––. "Training Design for Performance Improvement." In *Productivity in Organizations: New Perspectives from Industrial and Organizational Psychology,* edited by J. P. Campbell and R. J. Campbell. San Francisco: Jossey-Bass, 1988.

Campion, M., and C. McClelland. "Follow-Up and Extension of the Interdisciplinary Costs and Benefits of Enlarged Jobs." *Journal of Applied Psychology* 78, no. 3 (1993): 339–351.

Carlisle, K. *Analyzing Jobs and Tasks.* Englewood Cliffs, N.J.: Educational Technology, 1986.

Carnevale, A. P. *Human Capital: A High-Yield Corporate Investment.* Alexandria, Va.: American Society for Training and Development, 1983.

Carnevale, A. P., and E. Schulz. "Return on Investment: Accounting for Training." *Training and Development* 44, no. 7 (1990): s1–s32.

Cascio, W. F. *Costing Human Resources: The Financial Impact of Behavior in Organizations.* Boston: PAWS-Kent Publishing, 1987.

Clements, J. C., and B. M. Josiam. "Training: Quantifying the Financial Benefits." *International Journal of Contemporary Hospitality Management* 7, no. 1 (1995): 10–15.

Craig, R. L., ed. *Training and Development Handbook,* 4th ed. New York: McGraw-Hill, 1996.

Cullen, G., G. Sisson, S. Sawzin, and R. A. Swanson. "Training: What's It Worth?" *Training and Development Journal* 30, no. 8 (1976): 12–20.

––––––. "Cost Effectiveness: A Model for Assessing the Training Investment." *Training and Development Journal* 32, no. 1 (1978): 24–29.

Daily Telegraph, October 27, 1997. Davenport, T. O. *Human Capital: What It Is and Why People Invest in It.* San Francisco: Jossey-Bass, 1999.

D'Aveni, R. A., and D. J. Ravensscraft. "Economies of Integration Versus Bureaucracy Costs: Does Vertical Integration Improve Performance? *Academy of Management Journal* 37, no. 5 (1994): 1167–1206.

Demeuse, K. P., and S. J. Liebowitz. An Empirical Analysis of Team Building Research. *Group and Organizational Skills* 6, no. 3 (1981): 357–378.

Dixon, N. "The Relationship Between Trainee Responses on Participant Reaction Forms and Posttest Scores." *Human Resource Development Quarterly* 1, no. 2 (1990): 129–137.

Dooley, C. R. *The Training Within Industry Report, 1940–1945.* Washington, D.C.: War Manpower Commission Bureau of Training, Training Within Industry Service, 1945.

Edvinsson, L., and M. S. Malone. *Intellectual Capital: Realizing Your Company's True Value by Finding Its Hidden Brainpower.* New York: HarperCollins, 1997.

Fitz-Enz, J. *Human Value Management.* San Francisco: Jossey-Bass, 1990.

_____. *The ROI of Human Capital: Measuring the Economic Value of Employee Performance.* New York: Amacon, 2000.

Flamholtz, E. G. *Human Resource Accounting.* San Francisco: Jossey-Bass, 1985.

Geroy, G. D., and R. A. Swanson. "Forecasting Training Costs and Benefits in Industry." *Journal of Epsilon Pi Tau* 10, no 2 (1984): 15–19.

Gilbert, T. E. *Human Competence.* New York: McGraw-Hill, 1978.

Gilbert, T. F. *Human Competence.* Amherst, Mass.: HRD Press, 1996.

Gilley, J. W., and A. Maycunich. *Organizational Learning, Performance, and Change: An Introduction to Strategic Human Resource Development.* Cambridge, Mass.: Perseus, 2000.

Harless, J. *An Ounce of Analysis Is Worth a Pound of Objectives.* Boulder, Colo.: Marlin Press, 1971.

Harrison, M. I. *Diagnosing Organizations.* Beverly Hills, Calif.: Sage, 1987.

Hartz, R., R. Niemiec, and H. Walberg. "The Impact of Management Education." *Performance Improvement Quarterly* 6, no. 1 (1993): 67–76.

Head, G. E. *Training Cost Analysis.* Boulder: Marlin, 1985.

_____. *Training Cost Analysis.* Alexandria, Va.: ASTD Press, 1993.

Hendricks, K. B., and V. R. Singhal. *Does Implementing an Effective TQM Program Actually Improve Operating Performance? Empirical Evidence from Firms that Have Won Quality Awards.* Williamsburg, Va.: School of Business, College of William and Mary, 1995.

Holton, E. F. "The Flawed Four-Level Evaluation Model." *Human Resource Development Quarterly* 7, no. 1 (1997): 5–21.

_____. "What Is Performance? Bounding the Domain." In *Advances in Developing Human Resources: The Theory and Practice of Performance Improvement,* edited by R. Torraco. San Francisco: Berrett-Koehler, 1999.

Kaplan, R. S., and D. P. Norton. *The Balanced Scorecard: Translating Strategy into Action.* Boston: Harvard Business School Press, 1996.

Kearsley, G. *Costs, Benefits, and Productivity in Training Systems*. Reading, Mass.: Addison-Wesley, 1982.

Kirkpatrick, D. L. *Evaluating Training Programs: The Four Levels*. San Francisco: Berrett-Koehler, 1994.

Krohn, R. A. "Training as a Strategic Investment." In *Strategic Perspectives on Knowledge, Competence, and Expertise*, edited by R. Herling and J. Provo, 63–75. San Francisco: Berrett-Koehler, 2000.

Krugman, P. *Peddling Prosperity*. New York: Norton, 1994.

Kusy, M. E., Jr. *The Effects of Types of Training Evaluation on Support of Training Among Corporate Managers*. St. Paul: Training and Development Research Center, University of Minnesota, 1986.

———. "The Effects of Types of Training Evaluation on Support of Training Among Corporate Managers." *Performance Improvement Quarterly* 1, no. 2 (1988): 23–30.

Lyau, N. M., and D. J. Pucel. "Economic Return on Training at the Organization Level. *Performance Improvement Quarterly* 8, no. 3 (1995): 68–79.

Mattson, B. W. "Development and Validation of the Critical Outcome Technique." *Human Resource Development International* 3, no. 4 (2000): 465–487.

Mattson, B., L. Quartanna, and R. A. Swanson. "Assessing Management Development Programs with the Critical Outcome Technique. In *Implementing Evaluation Systems and Processes*, edited by J. Phillips, 211–227. Alexandria, Va.: ASTD Press, 1998a

Mattson, B. W., L. J. Quartanna, and R. A. Swanson. "Assessing the Business Results of Management Development Using the Critical Outcome Technique at CIGNA Corporation." In *Academy of Human Resource Development 1998 Annual Proceedings*, edited by R. J. Torraco. Baton Rouge: AHRD, 1998b.

Mattson, B. W., and R. A. Swanson. *Electronic Support for the Performance-Learning-Satisfaction Evaluation System*. Washington, D.C.: ISPI Press, 1998.

Mincer, J. "On-the-Job Training: Costs, Returns, and Some Implications." *Journal of Political Economy* 52, no. 5 (1962): pt. 2, 50–79.

Mooney, M. "Process Management Technology." *National Productivity Review* (autumn 1986): 386–391.

Mosier, N. R. "Financial Analysis: The Methods and Their Application to Employee Training." *Human Resource Development Quarterly* 1, no. 1 (1990): 45–63.

Murphy, B. P., and R. A. Swanson. "Auditing Training and Development." *Journal of European Industrial Training* 12, no. 2 (1988): 13–16.

Nicholas, S., and R. W. Langseth. "The Comparative Impact of Organization Development Interventions on Hard Criteria Measures." *Academy of Management Review* 7, no. 2 (1982): 531–542.

Ostroff, C. "Training Effectiveness Measures and Scoring Schemes: A Comparison." *Personnel Psychology* 44, no. 2 (1991): 353–374.

Parker, B. L. "Summative Evaluation in Training and Development." *Journal of Industrial Teacher Education* 23, no. 2 (1986): 29–55.

Peters, T. *Thriving on Chaos.* New York: Knopf, 1987.

Phillips, J. J. *In Action: Measuring Return on Investment.* Alexandria, Va.: ASTD Press, 1994.

_____. *Handbook of Training Evaluation and Measurement Methods, 3d ed.* Houston: Gulf, 1997.

Provo, J. "Measuring Human Capital." In *Strategic Perspectives on Knowledge, Competence, and Expertise,* edited by R. Herling and J. Provo, 76–90. San Francisco: Berrett-Koehler, 2000.

Robinson, D. G., and J. C. Robinson. *Performance Consulting: Moving Beyond Training.* San Francisco: Berett-Koehler, 1995.

Romanelli, E., and M. L. Tushman. "Organizational Transformation as Punctuated Equilibrium: An Empirical Test." *Academy of Management Journal* 37, no. 5 (1994): 1141–1166.

Rosentreter, G. E. "Economic Evaluation of a Training Program." In *Studies in Training and Development: Research Papers from the 1978 ASTD National Conference,* edited by R. O. Peterson. Madison, Wisc.: ASTD Press, 1979.

Rossett, A. *Training Needs Assessment.* Englewood Cliffs, N.J.: Educational Technology, 1987.

Rummler, G. A., and A. P. Brache. *Improving Performance: How to Manage the White Space on the Organization Chart.* San Francisco: Jossey-Bass, 1995.

Ruona, W.E.A. "Core Beliefs in Human Resource Development." In *Philosophical Foundations of Human Resource Development Practice,* edited by W.E.A. Ruona and G. Roth. San Francisco: Berrett-Koehler, 2000.

Schmidt, F. L., J. E. Hunter, R. C. McKenzie, and T. W. Muldrow. "Impact of Valid Selection Procedures on Work-Force Productivity." *Journal of Applied Psychology* 64 (1979): 609–626.

Schmidt, F. L., J. E. Hunter, and K. Pearlman. "Assessing the Economic Impact of Personnel Programs on Work-Force Productivity." *Personnel Psychology* 35 (1982): 335–347.

Schmidt, F. L., J. E. Hunter, A. N. Outerbridge, and M. H. Trattner. "The Economic Impact of Job Selection Methods on Size, Productivity, and

Payroll Costs of the Federal Work Force: An Empirically-Based Demonstration. *Personnel Psychology* 39 (1986): 1–30.

Schneider, H., D. Monetta, and C. Wright. "Training Function Accountability: How to Really Measure Return on Investment." *Performance and Instruction* 31, no. 3 (1992): 12–17.

Sleezer, C. M., ed. *Improving Human Resource Development Through Measurement.* Alexandria, Va.: American Society for Training and Development Press, 1989.

Sleezer, C. M., and R. A. Swanson. "Is Your Training Department Out of Control?" *Performance and Instruction* 28, no. 5 (1989): 22–26.

_____. "Measuring the Effects of an Organization Development Program." In *Measuring Return on Investment*, edited by J. Phillips, 223–234. Alexandria, Va.: ASTD Press, 1994.

Sleezer, C. M., R. A. Swanson, and G. D. Geroy. *Validation of the Benefit-Forecasting Method: Organization Development Program to Increase Health Organization Membership.* St. Paul: Training and Development Research Center, University of Minnesota, 1985.

Spencer, L. M., Jr. *Calculating Human Resource Costs and Benefits.* New York: Wiley, 1986.

Stern, P. *An Analysis of the Model for Evaluating HRD Programs from the Book: Forecasting Financial Benefits of Human Resource Development.* St. Paul: University of Minnesota Human Resource Development Research Center, 1995.

Swanson, R. A. "Industrial Training." In *Encyclopedia of Educational Research*, 5th ed., edited by W. H. Mitzel. New York: Macmillan, 1982.

_____. "Training Technology System: A Method for Identifying and Solving Training Problems in Industry and Business." *Journal of Industrial Teacher Education* 24, no. 4 (1987): 7–17.

_____. "Everything Important in Business Is Evaluated." In *New Directions in Program Evaluation—Evaluating Training Programs in Business and Industry*, edited by R. O. Brinkerhof, 44, 71–82. San Francisco: Jossey-Bass, 1989.

_____. "Demonstrating Financial Benefits to Clients." In *Handbook of Human Performance Technology*, edited by H. D. Stolovitch and E. J. Keeps, 602–618. San Francisco: Jossey-Bass, 1992.

_____. "Human Resource Development: Performance Is the Key." *Human Resource Development Quarterly* 6, no. 2 (1995): 207–213.

_____. *Analysis for Improving Performance: Tools for Diagnosing Organizations and Documenting Workplace Expertise.* San Francisco: Berrett-Koehler, 1996a.

_____. "PLS Evaluation System: Sales Communication Case Study." In *Academy of Human Resource Development 1996 Annual Proceedings*, edited by E. Holton, 718–725. Baton Rouge, La.: Academy of Human Resource Development, 1996b.

_____. "Demonstrating the Financial Benefit of Human Resource Development: Status and Update on the Theory and Practice." *Human Resource Development Quarterly* 9, no. 3 (1998): 285–295.

_____. "Demonstrating Return on Investment in Performance Improvement Projects." In *Handbook of Human Performance Technology, 2d ed.*, edited by H. D. Stolovitch and E. J. Keeps, 813–842. San Francisco: Jossey-Bass, 1999.

Swanson, R. A., and G. Geroy. "Economics of Training." Paper presented to the International Federation of Training and Development Organizations, Amsterdam, Netherlands, August 1983.

_____. *Forecasting the Economic Benefits of Training*. St. Paul: Training and Development Research Center, University of Minnesota, 1984.

_____. "Forecasting the Economic Benefits of Training." In *The 1987 Annual: Developing Human Resources*, edited by P. Goldstein. San Diego: University Associates, 1987.

_____. "Forecasting the Economic Benefits of Training." In *1987 Annual: Developing Human Resources*, edited by P. Goldstein. San Diego: University Association, 1988.

Swanson, R. A., and D. B. Gradous. *Performance at Work: A Systematic Program for Analyzing Work Behavior*. New York: Wiley, 1986.

_____. *Forecasting Financial Benefits of Human Resource Development*. San Francisco: Jossey-Bass, 1988.

Swanson, R. A., and E. F. Holton III. *Results: How to Assess Performance, Learning, and Perceptions in Organizations*. San Francisco: Berrett-Koehler, 1999.

_____. *Foundations of Human Resource Development*. San Francisco: Berrett-Koehler, 2001.

Swanson, R. A., D. R. Lewis, and C. M. Boyer. "Industrial Training and Economic Evaluation." *Program Development and Evaluation in the Private Sector*. Oslo, Norway: Norwegian National Academy of Banking, 1982.

Swanson, R. A., and B. W. Mattson. "Development and Validation of the Critical Outcome Technique (COT)." In *Academy of Human Resource Development 1996 Annual Proceedings*, edited by R. Torraco, 64–71. Baton Rouge, La.: Academy of Human Resource Development, 1997.

Swanson, R. A., and S. A. Sawzin. *Industrial Training Research Project*. Bowling Green, Ohio: Bowling Green State University, 1975.

Swanson, R. A., and C. M. Sleezer. "Training Effectiveness Evaluation." *Journal of European Industrial Training* 11, no. 4 (1987): 7–16.

———. "Organization Development: What's It Worth?" *Organization Development Journal* 6, no. 1 (spring 1988): 37–42.

Swanson, R. A., and C. M. Sleezer. "Determining Financial Benefits of an Organization Development Program." *Performance Improvement Quarterly* 2, no. 1 (1989): 55–65.

Thomas, B., J. Moxham, and J.G.G. Jones, J.G.G. "A Cost Benefit Analysis of Industrial Training." *British Journal of Industrial Relations* 7, no. 2 (1969): 231–264.

Tichy, N. "Managing Change Strategically: The Technical, Political, and Cultural Keys." *Organization Dynamics* (autumn 1982): 59–80.

Tichy, N. M., C. J. Frombrun, and M. A. Devanna. "Strategic Human Resource Management." *Sloan Management Review* 23 (1982): 47–61.

Torraco, R. J., and R. A. Swanson. "The Strategic Roles of Human Resource Development." *Human Resource Planning* 18, no. 4 (1995): 10–21.

Tribus, M. *Becoming Competitive by Building the Quality Company.* Kingsport, Tenn.: American Quality and Productivity Institute, 1985.

Ulrich, D. *Human Resource Champions: The Next Agenda for Adding Value and Delivering Results.* Boston: Harvard Business School Press, 1997.

U.S. Bureau of the Census. *Current Population Survey.* Washington, D.C.: U.S. Department of Commerce, January 1983.

Zemke, R., and T. Kerlinger. *Figuring Things Out.* Reading, Mass.: Addison-Wesley, 1982.

Index

About the Author

Richard A. Swanson is a professor at the University of Minnesota and senior partner in Swanson and Associates. Swanson is an internationally recognized authority on results assessment, organizational change, performance improvement, and human resource development. He received his doctoral degree from the University of Illinois. His undergraduate and master's degrees are from the College of New Jersey.

During Swanson's thirty years of experience, he has performed consulting work for several of the largest corporations in the United States and around the world. He has conducted study trips to Great Britain, Japan, Germany, the Netherlands, and South Africa.

Swanson has over 200 publications. Some of his recent books are *Analysis for Improving Performance* (1996), *Human Resource Development Research Handbook: Linking Research and Practice* (with Holton, 1997), *The Adult Learner 5th Edition* (with Knowles and Holton, 1998); *Results: How to Assess Performance, Learning, and Perceptions in Organizations* (with Holton, 1999); and *Foundations of Human Resource Development* (with Holton, 2001). Swanson is the founding editor of the *Human Resource Development Quarterly* and founding editor of *Advances in Developing Human Resources*.

Swanson is presently on the boards of directors of LifeFormations, Inc., the Minnesota Business Academy, and The Rite Stuff, Inc. He is past president of the Academy of Human Resource Development (AHRD) and in 1993 he received the American Society for Training and Development (ASTD) Professor's Network National Award for his "outstanding contribution to the academic advancement of human resource development" and the Scholar of the Year Award from the Academy of Human Resource Development. In 1995 ASTD/AHRD established the Richard A. Swanson Award for Excellence in Research. Swanson received the "Outstanding HRD Scholar Award" in 2000 from the AHRD and was inducted into the International Adult and Continuing Education Hall of Fame in 2001.